Magnetize Your Man

By Antia and Brody Boyd

Copyright © 2020 Antia and Brody Boyd at Find The One LLC

All rights reserved.
ISBN: 979-8633128024
MagnetizeYourMan.com

Table Of Contents

Introduction From Antia 1

Chapter 1: Overcoming Resistance 5

Chapter 2: The Attachment Codes 16

Chapter 3: The Art Of Feminine Allure 31

Chapter 4: Becoming the QUEEN 42

Chapter 5: Mastering Your Six Feminine Archetypes 56

Chapter 6: How & Where To Meet High-Quality Men 68

Chapter 7: Captivating Communication 83

Chapter 8: Owning Your Pleasure 99

Chapter 9: TRUST 110

Chapter 10: Setting Boundaries Without Guilt 123

Chapter 11: Vulnerability Without Weakness 136

Chapter 12: Courageous Confidence And Flow 147

Introduction From Antia

Right now I feel so grateful and blessed to be living this amazing life that I've been sharing with my loving, kind, strong, stable, trustworthy, and spiritual husband, Brody. I feel so cared for, safe, and loved in his arms.

We've been fortunate enough to travel the world together to amazing and gorgeous places such as Costa Rica, Mexico, Bali, Thailand, Australia, Maui, and Japan.

We also get to share our knowledge by speaking together on stages, at events, and in shows all over the world, such as Google, the Harvard University Faculty Club, America Trends, and ABC Radio.

But it wasn't always like this for me.

I grew up in an extremely emotionally distant household in East Germany before the wall came down. In my home, basic phrases like "I love you" were as common as Christmas and Thanksgiving happening on the same day.

In fact, my mother would constantly tell me not to bother her, and the core message that I learned from my father was "Who do you think you are?"

So I was forced to become Miss Independent at a very early age. My parents were having me go to the grocery store all by myself to pick up food for the family when I was only eight years old.

In fact, things soon got very hot politically, so my family ended up escaping to West Germany in the middle of the night.

All of this ended up affecting me on a deeper level than I realized even later on.

I grew up never feeling fully safe and secure in love, and I developed a hard shell of anxiety and an underlying lack of security when it came to love.

Fast forward several years, and what do you think I began to attract in my dating and love life?

That's right: emotionally unavailable men!

I began to feel the pangs of loneliness, frustration, sadness, and isolation that this pattern was causing. I very soon declared that I'd had enough.

I decided to risk everything, packed my bags, and headed to the United States to study personality psychology at the University of California, Berkeley. One of my goals was to finally uncover how my relationship with my parents directly correlated with my life-long struggles in dating and relationships—particularly attracting and keeping quality men.

While I did this, I also began studying everything that I could get my hands on in the areas of men, dating, personality styles, and interpersonal communication and relationships.

I went to dozens of workshops and training sessions on those subjects, read hundreds of books, and spent tens of thousands of dollars on my effort to turn my dream life and love into reality.

Because I was gaining so much valuable wisdom, I even decided to lead Soulmate Support Groups to help other women find success in their love lives.

And guess what? It worked ... for them!

I shared secrets, strategies, and systems to help dozens of other single women attract boyfriends, fiancés and husbands.

But it still wasn't happening for me.

I finally realized that the secrets, strategies, and systems weren't working for me because I was so stuck in my own patterns that I couldn't see my own forest for the trees. My struggle to find a partner was about me. My own deep programming, beliefs, and mindset were at the core of the issue. And that's when I finally decided to hire a one-on-one dating coach and mentor to help me get a handle on all of this.

After working with my personal dating mentor for only a few months and learning the Magnetize Your Man Method, I finally broke through my old personal patterns once and for all and started creating the lasting results that I was looking for.

I had finally learned how to trust myself and my heart, how to believe that this was all really possible for me, and know that I really could have what I wanted.

I learned how to step out of my comfort zone and take new, big emotional risks without fear, and how to say yes to letting new love and support flow to me. I learned how not to push it away subconsciously with my old cynicism, trust issues, and safety patterns that were keeping me alone. Shortly after that, I finally attracted my amazing, loving, and supportive husband, Brody, into my life, and I couldn't be happier.

We met in a spiritual/self-improvement support group in Hawaii where we were both living at the time. We connected on all levels right away shortly after meeting, and we got married in June 2014.

It's so good to feel loved, supported, and safe in the knowledge that we both care about and support each other fully in our lives together—and that we're committed to helping each other grow into the best versions of ourselves possible.

This entire journey of finally attracting true love into my life—where previously there had been only pain, struggle, and heartbreak—is why I became so passionate about helping single women. I wanted to help women of all ages and stages find the right man to share their life and be happier with ASAP. My goal was to help them leave the loneliness and frustration behind, and stop wasting time on emotionally unavailable men!

I'm looking forward to now helping YOU attract your ideal man and enter the archives of my great love success stories as well!

Are you ready for a whole new life and a whole new love?

It's all possible with the right new steps and strategies moving forward.

Chapter 1: Overcoming Resistance

"Most of us have two lives. The life we live and the unlived life within us. Between the two stands resistance."
– Steven Pressfield

What Is Resistance?

Resistance was one of the biggest blocks on Antia's journey to attracting Brody into her life.

It showed up in the form of pickiness and even cynicism, which was hidden under sarcasm.

Have you ever said to yourself, *All the good men are taken* or *I don't need a man*?

Antia had been single her whole life—she had a lot of first dates, but rarely any second ones. Her longest relationship lasted only two and a half months. So it's safe to say that her experiences had made her expect the worst from the future.

But her future turned out to be far different from her past. The goal of this book is to help you achieve tangible and life-changing results, too.

If you fully apply what you learn, you'll stop wasting time and energy on emotionally unavailable men and start attracting emotionally available men to share your life with—including the right man—without further fear, loneliness, and frustration.

How Does Resistance Get in Your Way?

One of the biggest challenges that may come up in your journey to attracting your dream man is resistance.

Resistance is that small and sometimes really loud voice inside your head that you hear right after you make a powerful decision that will change your life forever.

It's similar to what happens when you pick up a new weight set to begin exercising. As you start, you can feel the resistance of the weights as you lift them. That resistance is simply an indication that you haven't built the necessary muscle yet.

Resistance is just a small part of you that wants to keep you safe and secure. It will say things like:

I'm not ready yet.
What if it doesn't work out?
What if I can't trust him?
Oh my gosh, it's another book. What if it ends up just like all the other ones?

That voice comes from that small part of you—your ego—that's scared. It's trying to talk you out of change because it wants to keep you safe, but not necessarily happy.

Whenever you're changing, you have to face getting outside your comfort zone not feeling safe.

We like to think of resistance as an overprotective mother who says, "No, don't go out. Be careful."

But all this internal voice helps you achieve is comfortable misery. And you're not moving forward in your life.

What Does Resistance Look Like?

Resistance can express itself in many different ways because it has many faces.

You may prevent a new relationship from going further. For example, you could turn down a date for no good reason—or for a manufactured one. Or, when a date looks like it's heading toward more intimacy or an opportunity for you to be vulnerable, you might ask for the check so you can end the date.

Resistance can also show up as anger. Some women may respond with anger to avoid being vulnerable. Instead of opening up, they go into defense or attack mode.

Some women laugh and tell jokes as a way to keep themselves from feeling vulnerable. This mechanism allows them to avoid an intimate relationship that calls upon all of their emotions. And it keeps them from connecting with themselves and going deeper into their own emotional ecosystem.

Have you ever learned new information but failed to apply it to your life or take new action? If so, resistance may have been the culprit.

The common thread in all these examples is that resistance prevents you from making lasting changes in your life.

Don't Let Resistance Keep You From Your Treasure!

Learning is only information until you integrate and take action on it. Only then does it become a transformation that creates real results in your life.

So, make sure you're taking notes as you read this book. It's important to mark down the specific action steps that you're going to take right away and then do them.

"Don't stop three feet from gold." - Napoleon Hill

Once upon a time, there was a gold miner who was mining for gold until the vein dried up. He kept digging trying to find the gold again, but he couldn't. He eventually gave up. Months later, another prospector came along with a geological expert. They surveyed the land and found out that, because of a shift in the earth, the vein of gold was just three feet away from where the last gold miner had stopped digging. So, the second prospector bought the land, started digging in the right direction, and became a multimillionaire.

The closer you get to your goal, the bigger and louder resistance will get, and the more you may find yourself thinking, *It's not working. I've been doing this forever.* And you become very impatient.

Your brain will trick you. You'll be filled with unrealistic expectations. You'll think you know every little detail of the attraction process, and if things don't flow that way, fear kicks in.

Of course, resistance won't reveal itself to you for what it really is. Instead, it will invent excuses about why you can't continue to apply what you've learned, or why you suddenly don't have the time, resources, or energy for dating.

You may buy into the idea that this is reality. But in truth, it's just a part of you that's trying to navigate away from creating something new, something extraordinary and exciting. And it's all due to fear of the unknown.

Always remember: Your love zone is only as big as your comfort zone.

Every time you step outside your comfort zone, you'll meet resistance. If you don't know how to overcome it, you'll always stay in your comfort zone. And you'll never have what you really want.

To overcome it, you need to maintain that tension you feel inside and move forward despite that resistance. Work and focus toward your goal of attracting the right man into your life and becoming the best and most attractive you that you can be.

If you can't maintain that tension and overcome it, you'll experience a rubber band effect in which resistance pushes you right back to where you started.

The Four Styles of Mastering New Life Skills

There are four ways that women approach mastering new life skills. And all four apply to learning how to attract the man of your dreams:

The Dabbler: She's is the serial dater. No man is ever good enough for her, and she moves from date to date and opportunity to opportunity without going deeper into any of them. She attends events and workshops or even signs up for programs, but she doesn't show up consistently or do the work required. The Dabbler goes from one relationship to the next. She grows and discovers deeper intimacy along the way, but, at some point she feels resistance. That's when she says, "I'm out. I'm moving on to a new relationship." The heat in the oven of transformation just gets too hot for her.

The Hacker: She dates, but she stops putting the effort into the relationship after a period of time. She takes the approach that "men should just love me for who I am, flaws and everything." So she doesn't try to really be her best version of herself or create the best relationship possible. As a result, her relationships flatline and men leave her out of boredom and monotony. Sometimes she loses interest and passion herself and lets things fizzle out. She stays in mediocrity forever.

The Obsessive: When she hits resistance, she simply says, "I'm going to break through this resistance. I'm going to push even harder." So she pushes ... and then she cracks. She eventually burns out because it's just too hard to keep pushing against the resistance. She's not working with the resistance and isn't pacing herself. That could lead to her finding a guy she likes and trying to force things to work. She ends up compromising on her values, standards, and self-care.

The Master: When she starts learning a new skill, she starts growing. Eventually, however, she hits some resistance and plateaus. Most of her path will be on a plateau where she continues to show up, take action, work through resistance, and practice what she's learning in this program. In a relationship, this style looks like starting to see a man who's likely a great fit and experiencing the natural bumps that occur in a relationship. However, she works through those patiently and persistently, showing up consistently, improving herself and her skills, and giving things a real shot before moving on only if absolutely needed.

The Cycle of Plateaus and Growth

When Antia was single, she experienced lots of plateaus, also known as "dating deserts." Even though she had nights of absolute loneliness, she taught herself to make the most out of the plateau. She came to understand that the quieter it is on the surface, the more growth is occurring under the conscious awareness.

So she used the time to work with her dating coach, attend workshops, volunteer, and increase her horizon in different areas of life. She came to know that after every ebb there comes a flood, so she used times of loneliness to prepare for the next flood.

Eventually, you, too, will have a growth spurt followed by a plateau. This cycle will continue. In this process, you can properly manage resistance by working with it and continuing to grow and practice even when the resistance comes up.

What Does Resistance Look Like in Dating?

Resistance shows up in different phases of the dating journey.

Some women set up their dating life for failure from the get-go. Either their expectations are so outrageously high that no man could fulfill them, or they continue to say yes to the wrong men and stay in a loop of disappointment.

When Antia was dating, she interacted with one unavailable man after the other. So she grew used to distance, irregular contact, yearning for more attention, and an overall sense of insecurity. When Brody, a completely secure man, came along, he brought Antia a different set of experiences—experiences different from what she was used to. Her system didn't register the dynamic she had with him as love, so she got confused. Since a confused mind says no, she pushed Brody away. She even broke up with him because she truly felt she was losing control. The relationship felt too easy and calm to her.

Of course it did!

When you hit a plateau, don't buy into your friends' or parents' belief systems and opinions. Ask yourself, *Where am I going deeper? How am I getting ready for the next level?*

When you're in a plateau, you're growing roots so you can grow higher. If you never hit a plateau, your roots won't be deep enough to sustain all the growth.

It's the same concept as the one you probably know from exercise. If you don't work on your stability, you'll get injured very quickly when you're actively exercising and growing your strength.

An emotional plateau works the same way. It's when your subconscious is stretching, maintaining, and repairing so it's ready for the next round of emotional growth and activity.

Sometimes resistance, that persistent inner gremlin, tries to talk you out of things that you're committed to—things that are important to you. In that moment, a stronger part of you is going to show up. This is the Queen that lives inside you. She's wise and strong. She knows what you're committed to and what's really important to you.

Meet Your Inner Queen

The Queen inside you is going to hear the voice of resistance and say, *Thanks for sharing. But I'm committed to going for what I really want, and I'm saying yes to that vision of what I really want.*

This is your life. You only get one go-around, so make the rest of your life the best life possible. Don't give in to fear. Don't give in to doubt that will only keep you where you've been.

This is a chance to move forward, and your internal Queen will help you. That commitment energy is what's going to help you keep moving forward on this path to receiving what you truly want.

You have many different parts inside you. And that's what we mean when we talk about capacity. You have a lot of resources inside that you can use for support and motivation as you move forward.

You can always have a conversation with all the different parts inside of you. You may ask powerful questions, such as, *How can I integrate all of my parts so they're always moving forward and my thoughts, words, and actions are in alignment?*

How This Book Can Help You

This book will challenge you to complete and practice homeplays designed to help you get past everything that's blocking you from your dream relationship.

For example, the homeplay on resistance will help you identify and work through your resistance to the experiences and opportunities that could take you where you want to go.

This book will also help you identify what you're doing to prevent your ideal relationship from arriving.

The important place to start is to ask yourself the following kinds of questions:

> If you're attracting emotionally unavailable men, ask yourself: *Where am I emotionally unavailable? Where am I unavailable in general?*
>
> If you're attracting men who flake on you, ask yourself: *Where am I flaking?*
>
> If you attract men who don't want to commit, ask yourself: *Where am I not committing fully? Where am I not showing up fully?*
>
> If a man's not showing up, ask yourself: *Where am I not showing up fully? Where am I not committing fully?*
>
> If a man's not being open and vulnerable with you, ask yourself: *Where am I not being open and vulnerable?*
>
> If a man is having intimacy or trust issues, ask yourself: *Where am I having intimacy issues? Where am I having trust issues?*

Also, ask yourself:

What do I want?
Who is my ideal man?
What is my ideal relationship?
Why do I want it?

When you think about the answers, go even deeper so you can get to the core benefits of what you want rather than just the features. What are the real benefits you want, and how do you really want to feel? Do you want to feel alive, beautiful, supported, cherished, and safe?

How are you resisting?

What are you afraid of?

How can you start to face those fears head on?

What plans can you put in place to creatively overcome those fears?

How will you move forward, out of your comfort zone, into the world, towards the life you truly want?

You're already well on your way to attracting your ideal man into your life. It's possible, it's doable, and you deserve this. You're a Queen.

We deeply honor and acknowledge you for your high level of commitment, for saying yes to a happier and more fulfilled life, for being motivated, fully committed, and ready to step out of your comfort zone.

You're ready to say no to the old reality, suffering, and wasted time. You've begun the journey of making the rest of your life the absolute best of your life!

We can't wait to add your amazing success story to our collection. We're excited to learn what action steps you're going to implement to create the loving, long-term, and supportive relationship of your dreams.

You've got this! We're here for you and we believe in you. So let's do this!

Chapter 2: The Attachment Codes

To start diving into your new love journey, we're going to talk about something that Antia became very passionate about during her journey to love: the attachment styles.

There are three primary attachment styles in love. Knowing them allows you to uncover your own working model and understand which styles work for you and which are counterproductive.

Plus, you'll stop sending incongruent and mixed signals. As a result, you'll be able to finally stop attracting emotionally unavailable men.

The three attachment styles are:

Secure
Avoidant
Anxious

They're derived from research on attachment styles and attachment theory by psychologists John Bowlby and Mary Ainsworth.

To better understand them, picture a spectrum. On the left side of the spectrum, you have anxious. On the right side is avoidant. In the middle, you have secure.

The Strange Situation Study

The concept of attachment styles originated with a study at UC Berkeley.

Mary Ainsworth, a researcher at UC Berkeley, conducted the Strange Situation study, in which she observed the behavioral pattern of young children in relation to their mothers. She took toddlers (18 to 24 months) into a room with their mothers, let them spend a short time together, then had the mother leave.

The researchers looked for each child's response to the mother's departure, and, more importantly, his response to the mother's return.

Here's what the researchers concluded:

The anxiously attached child was upset when the mother left.

The securely attached child was also upset when the mother left.

The avoidant child didn't react at all on the outside even though his heart rate showed distress when the mother left.

But the children's responses to the mothers' return reveals the biggest contrast between secure and anxious attachment styles.

The anxious child was somewhat happy when the mother returned but was also very upset and attempted to push the mother away. So, it's a very incongruent pattern. On the one hand, he needs the mom for survival, so he's happy that she's back. But the child also resents her, as if to say, *I need you, but you left me alone. You abandoned me and now I want to punish you.*

In this case, the mother gave inconsistent feedback to her child's cues. In other words, when he cried or wanted food, he received an inconsistent response. As a result, life became a gamble for the child.

Anxious Attachment

When Antia was single, she lived in anticipation land. She would start visualizing herself walking down the aisle with a man after their first date. Each of these men would tell her that she was the one he'd always wanted, and then he'd drop her like a hot potato soon after.

Every time a man complimented her or mentioned that it would be fun to travel or do something with her sometime, she would start telling herself stories about her future and making interpretations of the man's words and actions.

In short, she created a false certainty by filling in the blanks herself.

This is a classic example of the anxious attachment style.

Women with anxious attachment styles are drawn to emotionally unavailable men until, or unless, they heal their emotional wounds. This is because emotionally unavailable, or avoidant, men give these women a familiar feeling of anxiety. They make anxious women feel like they're gambling and never know what will happen next.

So if you have an anxious attachment style, you'll attract plenty of uncertainty. You'll also experience in your brain a chemical addiction to that emotional pattern of highs and lows that's built on uncertainty.

In other words, you'll want to be with men who make you feel like a million fireworks are going off inside you. It feels exciting and there's a lot of tension, passion, and drama. But it's only an illusion.

In reality, the synapses in your brain are firing off "danger, danger, danger." And you're addicted to that danger because it makes you feel alive. Any other relationship—especially secure ones—seem boring or uninteresting to your emotional system—and definitely to your nervous system.

The anxious attachment style isn't about feeling safe. It's actually about feeling very unsafe.

The child feels very unsafe when the mom doesn't feed him. But he also feels hopeful because of the anticipation that she'll feed him next time.

If you have an anxious attachment style, you'll do the same thing with men. You're constantly living in the future. You may have an expectation that if you text with a smiley face, or maybe if you can just learn to be more patient, he'll come around. You can't accept the uncertainty of your situation with him, and you may even start fantasizing about how your first name will sound in front of his last name!

You likely already see yourself walking down the aisle. But your true desires will never be met. As a result, your anxiety goes absolutely through the roof! It can turn into an extremely traumatic experience for you because the relationship and its connected anxiety can become so intense. It causes you to become more and more agitated and react to thoughts in your head instead of to reality.

If you have an anxious attachment style with men, you're also likely to be a people-pleaser. You'll suppress all your emotions because you need to make sure that you're "acting decently with the man." You certainly don't want to rock the boat with him because you sense that he's already hot, cold, and indecisive about you. You just want to make sure that everything stays smooth, and that's a big challenge!

Antia knows this so well because this was her when she was dating.

It all comes down to one basic thing: The way you were treated as a child is going to have an influence on your adult patterns with men. If you have an anxious attachment style, you're going to attract mostly unavailable and avoidant men. This is one of the biggest challenges women struggle with in dating: They believe that they're unworthy of love.

Avoidant Attachment

In some ways, an avoidant attachment style is the complete opposite of the anxious. But it still originates from an insecure paradigm. Emotionally avoidant people push others away, close off their hearts, and avoid intimacy.

Something interesting and heartbreaking happens with an avoidant child in the Strange Situation Study. When the mother leaves, the child simply doesn't care. He just continues to play. There's a researcher in the room, so the child continues exploring. He still doesn't really care even when the mom returns.

Why?

He has already detached from the mother emotionally because he didn't get enough attention from her in the first place.

An avoidant believes that they can't trust people to fulfill their needs.

It's terrible to consider how this can happen. The child may go through a phase of absolute devastation in the most horrific way emotionally, so he detaches for survival reasons.

The child knows the mother isn't going to be there in the way he needs, so he makes a subconscious decision not to rely on her. He won't love her. The child has learned that he can't rely on anyone but himself.

When it comes to dating and romantic relationships, this style is absolutely disastrous. Every time an avoidant person gets too intimate—when love, closeness, and affection are exhibited—they're repelled and freak out.

Remember, an avoidant person developed their style because they were detached from their mother. They realized that when they were the closest and most intimate with their mother, they were abandoned.

These grown adults feel their survival mechanism kicking in the closer they get to intimacy. This leads to inconsistent communication with romantic partners. Avoidant people find themselves getting close, then withdrawing. At that point, they seek closeness again, but then back off once again. Usually, they're more withdrawn than their partner as soon as things get more emotionally intimate. They can't withstand the heat of intimacy.

A relationship with an avoidant has a lot of push and pull. It becomes hell on Earth because the avoidant isn't eager to feel loved at a deep level.

There are many reasons why this happens. Among them are the fear of being controlled and the fear of being left alone, which cause them to avoid their emotions and not listen to their heart. They want to avoid getting too emotional.

People who are avoidant believe they can rely only on themselves. So if you're avoidant, you believe that you're on your own. You don't care about what other people want from you. If they ask you to call them at a certain time, you don't care. You don't feel responsible for anybody other than yourself.

Brody knows this well. He used to be a bit more on the avoidant end of the spectrum but had healed much of this before he met Antia.

Brody grew up in a household where he felt his mother controlled him somewhat. Although she had good intentions, his avoidant tendencies came from a feeling of being smothered and trapped. When he was growing up, he started closing his heart off to women and attempted to stay away from people in general because he didn't want to feel controlled.

There are ways you can help a man feel safe so he can get close to you without having to worry that you're going to trap, control, or criticize him. You can help him feel safe so he can feel secure and open up. It starts with being curious about his past and why he became the man he is.

Secure Attachment

This attachment style, which sits in the golden middle of the spectrum, is the goal. Ideally, it's where we all should be headed because the middle is where we find balance.

Here's what happened with the secure infant in the Strange Situation Study: He was upset when mom left, but he was easily soothed when she returned.

This was because he trusted his mom. He knows she's always there for him and has a healthy attachment to her. This is why he was upset when the mother left. This kind of attachment comes, of course, from consistent nurturing, paying attention to the baby's needs, and constant affection and attention.

When it comes to romantic relationships, this style results in consistent communication, the ability to express emotions easily, and the capacity for loving intimacy.

In short, people with secure attachment styles aren't concerned about love. They have very little fear and few insecurities about it because they walk through the world knowing that they're worthy.

The secure attachment style is your aim.

The King/Queen Matrix

We like to present the different attachment styles in an illustration we call "The King/Queen Matrix":

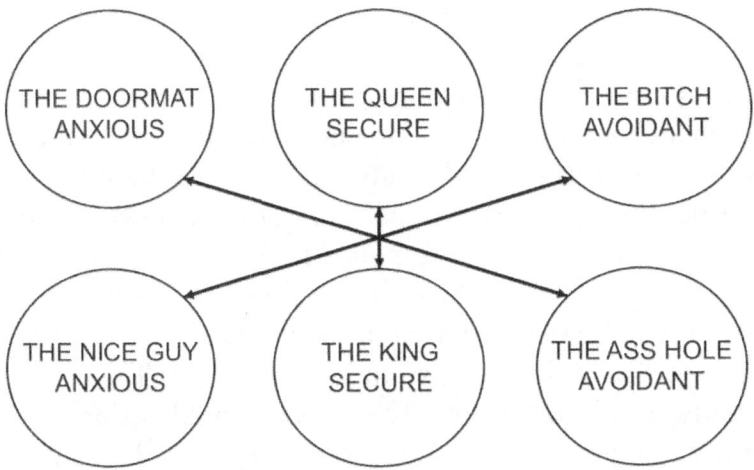

On the left side, you have the archetype of the Doormat. On the right side is the Bitch. In the middle, you have the Queen.

The Doormat tends to be on the anxious side, and the Bitch tends to be on the avoidant side. But the middle is your ideal because that's where you become the secure Queen.

What we're focusing on here is your ability to open up your heart and get close to a man without pushing him away or pulling him in. You want to avoid having to trap him. You want to stand next to him without leaning against him.

That's the key to becoming the secure woman: It's going to allow the man to see you as his queen!

The goal is to allow him to feel safe coming closer to you emotionally. The secure attachment style allows intimacy to develop between the two of you, but it also enables you to set boundaries with an open heart.

Now let's talk about the dynamics between two of these styles.

Anxious + Avoidant

Because of the law of polarity, we all tend to attract our opposite. So, anxious people will attract avoidant people, and avoidant people will attract anxious people.

When an anxious woman attracts an avoidant man, the dynamic is painful for her because all her worst nightmares come true. She wants to have her needs met, but she's with a man who believes he's not responsible for meeting anybody's needs.

Do you see how devastating this can be?

You see this dynamic play out all the time on TV—especially on *The Bachelor*. The drama capitalizes on the woman's anticipation (*One day he will love me*). But the moment she gets closer to the avoidant man, he pushes her away (*I'm out of here*).

His survival mechanism and behavior kick in when she comes too close, while her survival mechanism engages when he pushes away. It's a total disaster and becomes a cat-and-mouse kind of game in which she gets close, he pulls away, she pulls away, he gets close, and so on.

Anxious and avoidant people are attracted to each other because of this dynamic. It keeps them attracted to each other but won't allow them to get too close. As the tension goes away, one person wants to pull away. They're never happy.

You may think that you're attracted to a man who's pulling away, being distant, or avoiding. But actually you're running the same old attachment pattern from your childhood experiences.

It's not attraction. It's a combination of anxiety and uncertainty. In fact, we created a name for it: *attraction-xiety*.

Both of these feelings come from a fear under the surface that you're not going to be loved. Fear that you're missing out. Fear that he may actually be able to give you the love that you never had from your father or mother, or the hope that you may finally have it and be able to close the loop of childhood trauma.

Your brain interprets all of these emotions as attraction and chemistry because it's what you experienced when you were younger—when people you were closest to you failed to give you love.

This mix of fear, anxiety, and uncertainty is what you learned love was.

If you can learn the distinction between what love is and what you've come to think it is, your life will change forever. You'll want to move toward a relationship with a secure-style partner because it will feel safe. It will soothe your system.

The challenge will be that this secure relationship might feel boring to your system. It may feel bland because it won't make all those neurons fire. It won't ignite all the fireworks and create those old patterns you've grown to know.

But you have to remember that in a relationship with an avoidant your neurons fire off because your subconscious is excited and says, *This is love because it's like the love I experienced in childhood.* It doesn't matter if it's dysfunctional. You think this is what love is for you.

When you find yourself in a relationship with a secure man, you may hear yourself say, "I don't know if I have attraction or chemistry with him." But remember that you're still in the process of rewiring your pattern and attachment style.

Don't rush to judge a relationship as unexciting or lacking attraction. It takes time to be excited about a man who's healthy for you! It's important to know that when you move toward secure love, your body isn't firing off and you won't be crazy excited.

And that's a good thing!

The only way to create a happy, fulfilling, loving, relationship that lasts is to get as close as you can to that secure place inside you so that you'll attract a securely attached man.

If you're a secure Queen, you'll attract a secure King. Remember, anxious tends to attract avoidance, and avoidance tends to attract anxious. But secure tends to attract secure.

When you grow more secure within yourself and understand the dynamics that have been going in your dating life, you're going to attract men who are secure. Even men who were more avoidant or more emotionally unavailable in the past will begin to feel safer being secure with you because you're secure. They'll move closer to intimacy. It will feel safer for them to be intimate with you in an emotional way, commit to you, and love you for life.

So, being truly secure is the key to having a happy, loving, long-term relationship. It's going to be uncomfortable in the beginning. That's because whenever you do anything new to get new results, you have to step out of your comfort zone. So, it's going to feel weird and you're going to feel like you're not really interested in the man. You might suspect the relationship isn't real or that the two of you don't have chemistry.

But what's really happening is you're moving past your old patterns to get to a secure place. You're forging the path to a loving relationship.

Homeplay: Feeling and Being Secure

So what do you do if you have an anxious attachment style? How do you get to secure? This homeplay is going to help you get there.

For Anxious Attachment

First, understand that a woman with an anxious attachment style is very other-focused. As a child she thinks, *I need to seize every opportunity because I don't know when Mom's giving me food or love. I need to predict it as much as I can.*

When she grows up, she does the same with men.

If this is you, your job now is to bring the energy back to yourself and learn how to self-source. It's really about asking yourself how you can create an emotionally satisfying experience for yourself first and foremost.

Before Antia met Brody, she dated a guy who had a sailboat. Everything was fantastic and they went out on the water all the time. One Sunday he asked her to go out with him on his sailboat. But she had an epiphany: Although she felt wonderful when she was with him, she knew he couldn't be the source of that feeling. If she couldn't create that feeling for herself when she wasn't with him, then she was codependent. Codependency is very unhealthy, and the relationship would not end up going well. So, she opted out of the sailboat outing.

Part of your challenge will be to opt out of some opportunities with men for a while. You need to see that you're the source of love, power, and happiness—love is coming through you and not from the men.

Rather than approaching dating and relationships like there's emptiness that you need a man to fill with love, we're taking the approach we call "self-sourcing" or "resourcing." Find creative ways to fill yourself up with those things that you're hoping to get from a man—love, approval, validation, security, happiness—so that you become the cup that flows over.

When you do, you'll start to draw men to you because you'll be overflowing with things men want from you. And what's even better: All those good emotions mean that you'll be happy while you're waiting for your ideal relationship to come along.

Working with a dating coach who can provide additional support and has your best interests in mind can really help you to break out of your old anxious attachment pattern.

Here are some additional ways that you can become more secure in your dating:

Set boundaries and say no even if you're not used to that. Give yourself what you want to receive. For example, Antia bought herself flowers and went out on dates by herself, which was really important for her.

Make yourself a favorite dinner that you would normally make for someone else. This is powerful and affirms your self-worth.

Take yourself out on a date. Go to a movie by yourself. Get dinner by yourself. Have a candlelit dinner by yourself. Build a relationship with yourself and fall back in love with YOURSELF! Antia went wedding-dress shopping for her future wedding. She even gave herself an engagement ring. Be creative and have fun with it. Write yourself a love letter! Paint your story from different perspectives.

For Avoidant Attachment

Women with the avoidant attachment style constantly dismiss reality and don't see that men are already doing some of the things that they would normally appreciate. They may dismiss a man's gestures, saying, "Well, he just sent me a birthday card, whatever." They don't acknowledge kind behavior because they're avoiding intimacy.

If this is you, take a deep breath and seek out intimacy. The goal is to seek out a more intimate conversation with your partner—but be sure to explain that you still need some space. For example, Brody told Antia when they began dating that he was afraid of being trapped in the relationship. So, to let Brody know that she honors his need for freedom, Antia said, "With this ring, I set you free" as part of their wedding vows.

Express your fears. What feelings do you have when you think about commitment? The key is to be consistent: Ease yourself into feeling safe in intimacy.

It's very interesting because the need for safety is what the anxious attachment style needs as well.

We'll Help You Meet in the Middle

Secure is exactly the middle point between anxious and avoidant. So the more you move toward secure, the more you'll attract a man, possibly an avoidant, who's also moving closer to secure.

That's what happened to Brody and Antia. Brody wasn't completely secure when Antia met him, but Antia had taken the time to work on herself. Brody and Antia held hands and walked the rest of the way to secure together.

If you're already on the avoidant side and have a fear of commitment, you could have what's called the anxious-avoidant style. If this is you, you push men away and are anxious about them at the same time.

If you have any avoidant tendencies, we'll teach you how to get rid of them. We'll show you ways to become more comfortable with intimacy and commitment. This will help you ease into a more secure balance so that you can feel safe being close to quality men.

And if you're already secure, that's great! We'll help you become even more secure and at peace with yourself. We'll show you how to love yourself, become whole, be more comfortable with intimacy, and feel safe with commitment. You'll learn how to take the steps that will bring you more fully into alignment.

You can become fully secure. And when you do, you're going to attract more secure men to you.

Also, the men in your world will start acting more secure with you. They'll be more available and more accessible. They'll be less anxious or avoidant. Men who have been really needy with you or have overly pursued you should become more relaxed and secure with you.

It doesn't matter where you are on the spectrum or how extreme on either side that you are at this moment. It's all about baby steps. It's not about feeling bad about the past—it's about being grateful that you have and will utilize this knowledge now.

You can turn your life around going forward and do things differently starting today.

Our message is to love yourself wherever you are. There are pluses and minuses to every attachment style. But your goal is to become harmoniously secure. We want you to have the loving experience in your dating and romantic relationship life that you deserve for your own happily secure ever after!

Chapter 3: The Art Of Feminine Allure

When Antia was lost in the jungle of never-ending first dates, she had no clue that the secret to magnetize Brody didn't lie in her wealth, successes, or competence.

It actually was in her femininity.

But Antia resisted femininity. She believed that being feminine would turn men off and repel them. As it turned out, nothing could be further from the truth.

In this chapter, you'll learn how to draw a man to you like a magnet so that he can't help himself falling in love with you.

The secret lies in feeding into his masculine archetype of "the Provider."

We all have archetypes inside. There are ways of being and aspects of yourself that you already possess, but you haven't necessarily stepped into them for one reason or another.

Those archetypes create polarity with different flavors of expression. We'll show you how to create that interest, attraction, and "juice" to get a man interested in wanting to commit.

What Have You Suppressed?

First, it's all about being yourself and looking at what you've been suppressing.

When Antia first started her journey, she was suppressing her inner girl. When she lived in Germany, she had to be very competent and professional to be taken seriously. She always made sure that her dresses weren't too colorful and that she didn't make any jokes or unexpected remarks. She was constantly trying to be proper, well-spoken, and well-dressed. She refused to "color outside the lines." She thought that being big, bold, and bright was bad!

Sad, right?

Her journey returned her to her playful self. Today, Antia absolutely loves to wear dresses. And the more color, the better. (While writing this, she's wearing a very sparkly dress.)

It's all about the magic and allowing yourself to express your inner girl again. It might mean going to a playground and swinging on a swing to feel that excitement and carefreeness that you had as a little girl.

You may be thinking, *Oh my gosh, I'm forty-five years old*, or *I'm a grown-up woman. I can't do that. People will think I'm crazy, including myself.*

Congratulations, you're on the right track because your ego always tries to keep you in that place of safety and certainty.

This chapter's homeplay won't make you feel safe and certain. In fact, it will be quite the opposite. This chapter will help you add spice and variety to your life.

Why settle for one color when you can be the whole rainbow? Why be strict, rigid, and well-spoken when you can explore all the emotional expressions that come out of you?

Maybe you always wanted to write a song. It doesn't matter if you have a good voice or not. We know many women who speak on stage—even as keynote speakers—despite not having "a good voice." Why? Because they own who they are, and the audience loves that.

And men love that.

Men don't care about perfectionism. As a matter of fact, the more polished you are, the less attractive, the less magnetic, the less interesting you are for them.

The more corners, shapes, and unexpected turns you have, the more intrigue and allure you create.

Polarity

We're talking about principles of the masculine/feminine polarity.

The only thing that creates attraction, chemistry, or passion for a man is the difference between masculine and feminine energy.

Masculine energy is really strong; it's structured, polished, directional, and dominant. Feminine energy is flowing, free, joyous, receptive, and submissive. It's filled with a wide range of emotions.

Neither of these energies is better than the other. They're equally important. They're simply different, and that's what creates the magnetism.

This chapter covers how to create that polarity so that you can be your most receptive in your feminine flow. After all, that's what draws a masculine man and keeps him attracted over the long term.

All of us have masculine and feminine energies inside us. And this masculine/feminine polarity is so important.

But we're not talking about your career here. You can be in your masculine in your career. We're talking only about your romantic relationships. When it comes to relating to men, you want to tap into your essence as a feminine woman. You want to bring it to the forefront so you can draw men to you like bees to honey.

Little (Inner) Girl

One of the most powerful ways you can step into your feminine essence is to embrace your inner little girl. Remember exactly how you were when you were very young, and celebrate that joyful energy. If you can't remember, look at little girls around you. Look at all their playfulness and joy, then reconnect yourself to the flowy, frilly, and pink side of life.

It doesn't matter what your age is—you can still reconnect to that little girl inside you and bring her out. It will attract a man to you because men want to be your protector and hero.

The Protector's Role

Brody has coached men for over thirteen years. Being a man himself, he knows that each man in a relationship wants his woman to be happy. A man's self-esteem is tied to a woman being happy.

If he feels like he can't make you happy or like your strength and independence renders him unnecessary, his masculine self-esteem goes down.

Even if you can do things for yourself, let him do things for you so he can feel like your hero.

If you don't need him, his masculinity shrivels. In the end, the two of you will become roommates or best friends, but you won't have any of that attraction. He'll eventually leave the relationship or look for a woman who does need him and values his masculinity.

Be the Unknown

Spiritual author and teacher Don Miguel Ruiz says, "We are the mystery to ourselves."

How can you continue to discover yourself? When you uncover yourself in the most playful, silliest, most outrageous ways, your man will be intrigued because what you reveal will be unexpected. And that surprise will be the spice in your relationship. Expect the unexpected, the unpredictable, and the X-factor, so to say.

Ask yourself in the morning, *How can I be even more of a mystery to myself? How can I step even more into the mystery of myself? What have I not uncovered?*

Example From the Boyd Household

Once they moved in together, Antia would go into Brody's office and jump up and down and do a little dance. Then she'd go back into her office and work. This jumping break allowed her to release a spontaneous outburst of joy.

Whatever it is that you want to do, it doesn't have to take a lot of time.

Surprise your man. Do something different. Surprise yourself. We know that part of you is thinking, *Are you out of your mind?*

The answer is, yes! We are! And we want you to be, too. You should strive to be totally out of your mind and into your body, into your joy, into your passion, into your self-expression, and into who you really are. When you're authentic, you can't predict yourself because your authentic self isn't linear. It's invisible and unpredictable.

When you pull out that little girl energy, the man's protective instinct that wants to take care of you is awakened. He'll feel like, *Oh my gosh, I love this woman. I can take care of her, I can see myself being with her for a while and I want to invest in her, do things for her, and protect her.*

He'll start to fall in love with that little girl part inside you.

So, if you're walling off that part of you, you're sending signals that you're strong and don't need a man. And the man won't be able to feel those protective, providing feelings for you.

Be a little more vulnerable and ask for help. It's powerful!

When my client Vanessa started to allow men to do her little favors. Her whole world changed. Let him open the door for you.

Then thank your man with your joy, your passion, your open heart, and your smile.

When Brody and Antia walk somewhere, sometimes Antia skips like a little kid. If you've forgotten what that looks like, go to the playground and watch some little girls to see how carefree they are. They don't worry if something makes sense or not. They listen to their body and connect to their higher self. They enhance the moment.

Being feminine is all about enhancing the moment. Being masculine is creating the actual moment, so that's the difference.

When you watch little girls, they have nowhere in particular to go. Instead, they seem to be thinking, *What else can I do with myself, right here, right now, or with my girlfriend?* They make up fun stories and roll on the ground. Spontaneity is a very typical attribute of the feminine.

Your spontaneous actions don't have to make sense. In fact, a lot of what we're talking about here isn't logical or rational. It's about doing something because you feel like it and you feel inspired.

What Keeps You From Being Spontaneous and Feminine?

You might feel like it's hard to be spontaneous and feminine because you:
  Don't trust men
  Don't trust yourself
  Feel needy
  Are afraid to lose yourself

A word of caution: Don't step into your little girl with the sole purpose of attracting your man. The reason why the inner girl attracts her man is that she dances with herself. She creates, sources, and generates all the joy and passion she needs by herself, even when she's alone.

That's right: She self-sources.

You can do this for the rest of your life. The man is just a bonus. That's a very important distinction. You shouldn't do any of this with the sole purpose of manipulating a man to be interested in you. Because if that's your intention, it's not going to work.

Your actions and behavior have to be authentic. You have to do these things for yourself.

Start to cultivate your spontaneous, joyful, and feminine side when you're by yourself. Before you go out, put on some fun music, like we talk about in Chapter 6. Maybe play some music you danced to as a kid—whatever music makes you feel giddy and playful and allows your fun side to shine.

Also, little girls don't take themselves too seriously. If something goes wrong, so what? Maybe you drove with your guy somewhere and he got lost because Google Maps isn't always reliable. Instead of getting upset or critical about it, try to have a good laugh. Try saying, "This is great. This is where we're going to have the sunset now."

Who knows: Maybe where you end up is actually better than your original destination.

The Power of Appreciation

Just a reminder about the power of appreciation: Always, reward the behavior you want to see more of.

Reward your man with acknowledgment and appreciation when he's being your hero, protector, and provider. Doing so encourages him to think, *Yes, I can win with her, I can make her happy and I want to do it more.*

He's going to want to continue doing those things. Plus, he's going to fall in love because he will realize that you're a woman who could make him happy. And that's what he wants to do with his life. He wants to feel valuable and happy.

Find the gratitude in your heart and say, "I appreciate you," or "Wow, not every man would do that." Tell him how his action or gesture makes you feel. That really puts an extra cherry on top for him.

Of course, appreciation and acknowledgement go both ways. So why should you go first?

Women naturally access their emotions more easily and organically than men. The more you access your emotions, the more your man can access his through you.

That's because you can feel your hearts talking to each other. It's proven that the cells of both hearts start to beat at the same rhythm and create an energy field together. There's an emotional intelligence that already exists, and the other person can pick up on it.

Beware of resentment or resistance. If you have thoughts like, *I can do it by myself. I don't need to give him appreciation*, try to uncover your blocks and find where the resentment originates.

Maybe there's an opportunity to forgive a male figure in your life, such as an ex-boyfriend, an ex-husband, a father figure, an uncle, or a brother. Look at what connotation the word *masculine* has for you. That's where the gold lies and where the healing starts.

It's so important to overcome the emotion that you're resisting and understand what you're feeling when you read these words: *Appreciate the man.*

If you think, *But, what about me? I want to be appreciated too*, maybe there's a wound for you there.

Maybe you haven't been appreciated in the past, so you think, *I'm not going first. He needs to go first. He needs to show me. I need to feel certain and safe first.*

That's an invitation to heal your unconscious, sabotaging patterns.

Emasculation

The other side of appreciation is emasculation. It is the opposite of appreciating a man. It's when you actually take away his masculine power.

In our Magnetize Your Man Six-Month Program, we see countless strong, successful, and independent women who emasculate men in subtle and not so subtle ways.

One of our clients would often tease a man on a date. If he dropped a napkin, she would say, "That was a stupid thing to do." Those little teasing remarks constitute criticism, and that's one of the biggest ways that women emasculate men. It's the opposite of appreciation because it cuts away at a man and makes him feel less like a man, less like your hero, and less like he can make you happy.

So, avoid doing things that subtly take away a man's masculinity, like:

Talking bad about him to others
Making yourself look superior to him
Purposely one-upping him
Showing contempt
Rolling your eyes over something he says or does
Talking down to him

Make sure that you're not running these destructive patterns as a protection mechanism to mask your own insecurities, to avoid being uncomfortable, to not show your vulnerability, or to escape being in your feminine.

This is the most important thing to remember: Reward the behaviors you want to see more of and ignore the ones you don't. That's all you really have to focus on.

When you reward him, you help him be more of your hero. And when he's free to be your hero, you'll feel safer being in your feminine and creating an amazing, juicy dynamic of passion and polarity. He'll start falling in love with you and be drawn to you.

Homeplay: Embrace Your Feminine

If you haven't done this already, a great way to practice the masculine/feminine dance is to actually dance! Try a dance class, whether it's salsa, ballroom, waltz, any of the Latin dances, blues, or, our favorite, West Coast Swing.

Practice being in that energy of playfulness but also being receptive and in your feminine. Be open and vulnerable and trust the man's lead. That's going to be great practice for being in your feminine. You'll slowly learn how to follow and be receptive.

It could be also a great way to meet some quality men, by the way.

Also, write down something that you could surprise yourself with. Maybe it's a place that you would never otherwise go to. Maybe you just take a different route home or eat at a different restaurant. Just really increase your exploratory drive. Healthy little girls have a very high exploratory drive, so do the same thing.

Stretch yourself and expand. Maybe go to an art gallery that you've never been to or try a motorcycle show. It really doesn't matter what it is, but the more outrageous it is and the more different from what you'd normally do, the better.

Practice getting into your little girl. Go to a playground or to the mall and watch kids playing. Watch the little girls as they play so that you can remember that energy.

Find ways to appreciate at least one or two men, even if they're just people at the grocery store. Thank a man for opening the door, thank him for reaching out, thank him for setting up the date or choosing a great restaurant. Appreciate that he's great at making decisions and say, "I love how smart you are. You're so great with this." Get used to showing your appreciation and get in the habit of it.

And remember to not criticize, act superior, or try to one-up.

It's about being protective of the man's heart. If you do just that one thing, he'll give you the kingdom.

Chapter 4: Becoming The QUEEN

Take your invisible crown, put it on your head, and say, "I'm a Queen."

In this chapter we talk about what the Queen is, what the Queen isn't, and how you can become the Queen.

You'll learn some practical tools and steps that you can implement on a daily basis. There are many ideas and concepts out there. We'll show you how to integrate them into actual, specific steps that you can measure and see results from.

For the longest time, Antia was what people call a "doormat." She was a people-pleaser and gave all her power away.

What does that mean? She said yes even when she didn't agree, and she stayed when she wanted to leave. She didn't voice her desires or opinions. Instead, she usually gave in to the desires of those around her.

This is not being the Queen.

We're talking about the Queen because we see so many women who give their power away and have no concept of what the Queen is. They don't understand the importance of self-respect and cherishing themselves.

We often hear the phrase, "I want my King." But guess what? If you want your King, you first have to become the Queen. And in order to do that, you have to know who the Queen is and why the Queen is important.

As the Queen, you'll become your best, most radiant, most magnetic self in your relationships. This will draw a man to you and allow him to respect you, fall in love with you, commit to you, want to keep you around for life, and strive to make you happy. When you're the Queen, your King will be addicted to making you happy. He'll want to be the best man he can be.

Does this sound enticing to you, or are you thinking, *That's a stretch, I can't even visualize it*? No matter where you are in your journey, just stay with us and trust the process.

Let's talk again about the concept of the King/Queen Matrix. On the opposite sides of the Queen are the Doormat and the Bitch. The Queen is essentially the middle ground because she's the perfect balance between the two extremes.

The Doormat

So many women are trained to focus on the other person, please the other person, make the other person happy, and not be selfish. So being the Doormat means giving your power away, bending over backwards, and turning yourself into a pretzel.

It's also about being anxious and insecure.

Often, the Doormat falls victim to narcissists, sociopaths, jerks, and unavailable men because these types of men sense that she's questioning herself. Doormats and these unhealthy types attract each other.

The Doormat also sends herself on guilt trips. She makes her happiness dependent on the other person's emotional state. If the other person is happy, she's happy. But, if the other person is sad, then she feels guilty and may wonder, *What did I do to make this person feel sad?*

She takes on an enormous sense of responsibility. The Doormat exaggerates her own ability because she thinks she has all the resources to make the other person feel better. This is a false perception because other people are responsible for themselves and their emotions.

The Doormat has to learn how to bring her energy and power back to herself. She needs to use her resources, faculties, creativity, and intelligence for herself and not for someone else. If she has some left over, then, yes, she can give it to another person. But she needs to take care of and fill herself up first.

Doormats tend to have the anxious attachment style, so they attract men who are more avoidant and don't get too close. It causes a dramatic relationship dynamic that's not fun. If you have an anxious attachment style, you probably know exactly how this feels.

In one of these relationships, the Doormat becomes drained and doesn't respect herself. She has to constantly break promises and ignore her integrity. She sells out herself and what she desires in an attempt to please the other person. We hear this all the time from women in the Doormat role: "I don't want to rock the boat."

Look, you're better off leaning in and becoming a boat-rocker.

If you're a Doormat, you're going to be a professional boat-rocker by the end of this chapter. You're going to shake up the other person and shift his whole paradigm because you're going to realize that your goal isn't to be liked. Your goal is now to be respected.

The Bitch

The Bitch is completely self-focused, so she's the opposite of the Doormat.

The Bitch didn't get the attention she needed from her parents, so she basically said to herself, *Screw the world. I'll take care of myself. I don't need anyone and no one should need me.*

Her heart is closed. She's unavailable to her emotions and feels that other people need to take care of themselves. She's not responsible for them or their feelings.

But, as strong as she sounds, she's not being true to herself. That's because we all want to be loved. Somewhere along the way the Bitch picked up the idea that it's safer to be disconnected from her emotions.

While the Doormat's strategy is to be liked and please everyone, the Bitch withdraws and distances herself. She's also condescending and thinks she's better than everyone else. But this is because she's compensating for her lack of confidence

She can be completely cold and logical. She's not kinesthetically connected to herself. But she doesn't care what other people think about her. She has already disconnected from everyone's opinions.

And that's the good part about the Bitch: She doesn't care what other people think about her.

As a result, she sets boundaries. She says no. If she's no longer interested in a date, she'll just get up in the middle of dinner and walk out. She never looks back and never wonders if her actions were right, wrong, or appropriate. She's just totally in her own world and focused only on herself, her happiness, her desires, and her needs.

The Bitch really respects herself. Other people don't necessarily like her, but they do fear her. She can be tremendously intimidating to men, which is why she tends to attract the nice guys who give all their power to her (the male version of the Doormat).

The Balanced Queen

But guess what? The Queen is the golden middle ground between the Doormat and the Bitch. The Queen is the perfect balance, taking the best from both.

In Buddhism we say everything's really about the golden middle. Oftentimes, you may think that your job in this life is to be the best helper and to be loved wherever you go. But you know what? Your job is to be balanced. That's because being balanced translates into expressing your authentic truth. And when you do, you'll become a magnet for positive things, experiences, and people.

That's what being the Queen does for you. The Queen is all about setting boundaries, but she's very congruent. She's intrinsically and extrinsically confident, meaning she doesn't have to use shields, compensation, or coping mechanisms. She always acts from compassion. The Doormat and the Bitch act from a place of fear.

When the Queen sets boundaries, she does it in a loving and firm way. When something is out of sync, she's compassionate with the other person because she knows that life is a balancing game.

She's also balanced within herself. She has a deep, intimate knowledge of all her parts: selfish, playful, innocent, wild, and fierce.

The Queen is the integration of the Doormat and the Bitch. She has the Doormat's good, soft, open heart and the Bitch's ability to set strong boundaries. Rather than being just liked or feared, the Queen is respected.

The Queen, the Bitch and the Doormat in Action

Let's say a man agrees to call a woman at a specific date and time, but then he doesn't end up calling when he said he would. Instead, he calls several days later.

The Doormat would probably pretend it never happened. When he finally calls, she says, "Hi, I'm glad to hear from you." She's nice about the whole thing because she's afraid he'll leave her because she's so anxious.

The Bitch, on the other hand, insults him or says, "I don't want to hear from you ever again. You're an asshole."

That is, if she even answers his call.

The Queen is the balance between those two strategies. Here's how that conversation would go with the Queen:

Queen: Hi, how's it going?
Man: I forgot about the call and I'm sorry.
Queen: Yes. Thanks for apologizing. I appreciate you calling and I was really hurt that you didn't call when you said you would. I felt like I lost some trust when that happened.
Man: I didn't mean to. I got caught up in work and I'm really sorry. Can I make it up to you? Let me buy you dinner.

The Queen accepts his willingness to make it up to her. They go to dinner and she's back to being the Queen because she let him correct his mistake.

This is an example of integrating both traits of the Doormat and the Bitch.

Another thing to note here is that the Queen was just quiet after she said what didn't work for her. She was very comfortable with uncertainty, tension, and silence because she's congruent inside herself. She can be quiet and let him prove himself to her. There's nothing she wants to evade, and there's no feeling she doesn't have compassion for. That man can then say to himself, *Wow. She's not kidding. She's taking herself seriously. I'd better take her seriously because otherwise I'm going to lose her.*

The Queen's heart is open, but she values herself, her feelings, her time, and her goals. She's kind (for the most part) but she sets a boundary and makes him aware of the impact of his actions. If he doesn't apologize or make up for it, she probably would say, "I'm probably just going to move on. It doesn't seem like we're really a great match." But she still gives him that chance to step up to the plate.

Another example is when a man asks a woman to drive to see him. The Queen tells him, "It sounds like tonight isn't such a great night for you logistically. Why don't we move it to another night when it's more convenient?"

What the Queen is saying between the lines is that she deserves to be treasured and cherished. And if that's not possible, then she's not available. She says it very gently and she gives him an out when she offers to reschedule.

In this same situation, the Doormat would probably do it. She would agree to pick up dinner and say, "Any other groceries or anything? Any dessert? I'm so grateful to get to spend time with you."

She would probably give him a massage afterward and maybe do his laundry, too.

In the same situation, the Bitch wouldn't even respond. She would insult him for even suggesting that she do all of that, which is really just attacking him. She won't give him a chance to learn, and she won't hold him to a higher standard and allow him to grow into it.

Instead, we can hear the Bitch saying, "I don't think so." This aggressive response puts the man on the defensive. That's because the Bitch tends to come from a place of, "I'm better than you." She attacks and turns the encounter into a competition. She feels like she has to be right at all times, which is not a healthy place to come from.

There are so many different examples of these situations. If you struggle with scenarios like these, it might be good to book a complimentary, fifteen-minute Magnetize Your Man Heart-2-Heart call with Antia. You can do that via MagnetizeYourMan.com. We'd love to hear about situations you've struggled with so we can explain the Queenly way to handle things.

How to Become the Queen

If you're coming from the Doormat side of things, you can move toward being the Queen by stretching into the Bitch's territory. Or, more accurately, what will feel to you like being the Bitch.

When you respond like the Bitch, what's actually happening is that you're getting more into balance and becoming the Queen. Remember: As the Doormat, you're on the far side of the Queen. By aiming for the Bitch, you'll land in the realm of the Queen.

If you've been more avoidant and more of a Bitch in the past—avoiding commitment and intimacy or being unkind to men—then you'll need to open up your heart, be more kind to men, give them more of a chance, and be more loving. When you do so, you'll retain your self-respect and strength, but also demonstrate an open heart and kindness. In other words, you'll be the Queen.

It's all about coming from a place of compassion and love rather than a place of attack. For the Doormat, being selfish is actually love because real love is saying no when things don't work for you. Do you know why that's love? Because it's authentic. Your honesty, your authenticity, and your truth are the biggest gifts of love that you can hand to anyone.

Knowing your truth is more important than being liked. You've got to lean into what you resist the most. If you're a Doormat, you have to start loving that Bitch part of you and let it heal you. You're not going to be a Queen if other people or their opinions still own you.

How to Embody the Queen

One of the principles of being the Queen is valuing yourself more than you value the other person.

This is going to be a challenge if you're coming from the Doormat side of things. But it's just like they teach when you're on an airplane: If the air masks come down, put your mask on first. You can't help others if you're suffocating and have nothing left to give of yourself.

It's the same in a relationship. You can't bring value to your man or to a relationship if you don't fill yourself up first.

Being the Queen is the only way to attract the King, and the King is the only one who can attract the Queen. Make an effort to become more of the Queen. Value yourself more so that you can attract a man who values you.

One way to do this is to set higher standards for both yourself and what you accept from men you're dating. It's about prioritizing what you need and setting rules.

How would you would like a man to treat you? What will you accept and not accept? Turn your answers into rules and raise your standards to value yourself. You're the prize and you're the catch. Write these affirmations down and repeat them often:

I'm a prize.
I'm a Queen.
I'm a catch.
Any man would be lucky to be with me!

From now on, men have to treat you like a Queen—however that might look like for you. It could be taking care of you, paying for dinner, pursuing you, committing to you, investing in you, reaching out, initiating things. If a man doesn't do these things, then you're gone. You won't accept anything less.

In fact, you'll open yourself up to another man who will do these things for you. Making and enforcing these rules will keep you from being the Doormat.

When you do raise your standards, though, you may have to let go of some men who aren't capable of rising to them. But don't worry: When you keep to your high standards, then quality, Kingly men who do respect, value, and admire you will take their place.

Men really are looking for a challenge. They don't want a woman who looks up to them all the time and puts them on a pedestal. Sure, they want to be your hero, but they also want that to be your choice. They don't want it to come from a place of neediness. They can tell the difference.

Quality men are attracted to a woman who comes from a place of intention and abundance, not scarcity. Although the Queen would never say this, she does believe this when it comes to selecting a man: *I can choose to not like you or approve of you right now because I don't need you.*

Everywhere you go, just tell yourself, *I'm a Queen*. That's first and foremost, even before you even leave the house. If you're more kinesthetic or visual, get a crown! (Antia has pink and purple ones.) Wear them at home just for the fun of it. Practice that energy and that mindset.

We have several clients who have crowns. They may not feel great about themselves in the moment, but they still put their crown on and say, "I'm a Queen." Affirmations are so important.

How Do Queens Behave?

We want you to study movies that do a really good job of representing the Queen.

The Age of Adeline is a great example. In the movie, Blake Lively is very Queenly. In one scene, she's pursued by a guy as she leaves a party. He wants to go home with her, but she chooses to leave by herself. She does this in such a Queenly way that she doesn't even have to say no to him. She just smiles at him and he knows that it's a no, but a warm no.

The Queen has a powerful aura: She's warm but strong in herself. You don't even have to say no. You're just energetically able to hold that boundary with people. The wrong men don't come close to the Queen because they know they're going to get rejected anyway. But Kingly, high-quality men are drawn to her like bees to honey.

The Queen holds her head up: When you walk, imagine that the back of your head is parallel to the wall behind you. We see a lot of women who look a little down. That's a Doormat-y way to be. Lift your head and chest a little bit, and look straight ahead. Always remember that you're meeting the next opportunity, the next amazing person, and the next amazing man. When you walk straight and with your head up, your heart is open.

And walk into a room with your womb first, with your hip tilted forward. This is really important. When women walk in with their womb first, men absolutely notice them.

The Queen doesn't make the first move: No more initiating with men romantically, period. This means no more hitting on guys or romantically approaching them, no more texting or calling them first. From now on, they text or call you first. If they don't, you're moving on and meeting other men.

You can still socialize and talk with men and even initiate conversations in a social environment. But keep it on a social, friendly, or professional basis. Let them move things in a romantic direction and ask you for a date or at least your phone number.

One of our favorite sayings is, "When in doubt, meet more men." If he's not stepping up, then you're meeting other guys—even going on dates—and you're opening yourself up to somebody even better. You're meeting better men until he steps up. If he doesn't, then someone else will.

The Queen lets the man treat: When you're going out to eat, he needs to buy the dinner and take care of things—such as opening the door for you and pulling your chair out. Don't be angry if he doesn't think to do these things. But at least have the mindset that you're the Queen and you expect these things to happen. Remember, you're the prize and he should feel fortunate to have a chance to spend some time with you.

The Queen doesn't get intimate until she's exclusive: Here's a general rule of thumb that will really help you: Don't have any form of sex with a man until you're in an exclusive relationship. And you can actually tell him that. If things are getting hot and heavy, you can say, "I don't do anything sexual until I'm in an exclusive relationship." And back that up with your body language.

Most guys get this, and they respect it because you're not saying that you'll never have sex with him or that you're waiting for marriage. You're simply saying that you're waiting to be exclusive. He's going to value you more. Plus, quality men will wait.

Here's another reason this rule is so helpful: It's very easy for a woman to become the Doormat when she's had sex with a man too soon. He didn't really work for it, and people tend to not value what comes too easy. So set that new standard.

The Queen speaks up: As soon as she feels the slightest discomfort or senses anything is off, the Queen says something. Even if she doesn't know what it is exactly, she just says something like, "Right now, this doesn't feel comfortable." Maybe the guy comes a little too close or called five minutes too late. Whatever it is, just make sure you speak to it.

Make it a practice to start with the small things so it doesn't lead up to bigger concerns that are much harder to work through. So for example, if a man calls you five minutes late, let him know that you noticed. If you let it go without commenting on it, you may start to secretly resent him or develop passive aggression.

Start with the small things to hone your intuition and teach the man that you're looking for the small distinctions and are really aware of yourself and your space. If he's a quality man, he'll respect you and your space.

But always acknowledge the good with the bad! For example, say, "I'm so glad you called! Thank you. But I noticed you called five minutes late."

The Queen loves herself: The Queen takes care of herself, believes in herself, looks at what's good about herself, and doesn't focus on the things she doesn't like. The Queen creates space for herself. She has a daily routine and does whatever it takes to maintain that space and balance for herself.

Homeplay: What Does Your Queen Want?

Write down the answers to these questions:

What are your new requirements for a relationship?

What are your standards for a man?

How does your ideal man treat you in a relationship?

What do you need from a man to keep you with him and prevent you from moving on to someone new?

Don't be too stringent or too loose with your answers. Set reasonable standards for what you're going to accept.

Are your new standards higher than ones you've had in the past? Good! Now you're valuing yourself as the Queen.

Chapter 5: Mastering Your Six Feminine Archetypes

Do you have moments when you think, *A part of me wants to go out, but another part of me wants to stay home and work?* This chapter is dedicated to these different parts of you, and we're actually going to put names to your six feminine archetypes.

Between the two of us, we've helped thousands of single women all over the world attract the right man. Through that work we've found that women have many conflicts inside, but so little awareness of the resources they also have within.

We all have different energies, or characters, inside us. These characters are called archetypes. Many of us make the mistake of identifying with one of those archetypes and thinking that it's all we are rather than just a part of who we are.

In reality, you have all of these archetypes inside you, and all of them can help you. The six primary archetypes for women are:

The Queen
The Lover
The Warrioress
The Priestess
The Little Girl

The Wild Woman

The goal is to understand how each of these is expressed and works uniquely for you. Some will be stronger than others. Your job is to get them all into a healthy balance.

When you do balance them, you'll be a fully empowered woman. That balance and empowerment will draw the right man to you like a moth to a flame. He'll see that you have range—that you're a healthy and psychologically integrated person. And he'll want in on the life and balance you've created for yourself.

Understanding these archetypes is also super powerful when you're dating. When you recognize your own archetypes, you'll able to see where the man is off or where he can strengthen his own archetypes.

The Queen

The Queen is powerful because, as we've already seen, she comes from balance and alignment. She's in her heart, not just in her head. She's not all willpower, but she's not all Little Girl. She comes from the true heart and unconditional love. This means she expresses all of her emotions. And she empowers people to bring out all of their emotions. She doesn't enable a victim mentality. Instead, she empowers people.

The Queen sets clear boundaries and is very good at delegating. If you're not embracing your Queen archetype, then you don't really have direction and you're not being a manager. You'll just have all the other archetypes going all kinds of directions.

Imagine you're on a ship and your crew doesn't know what their jobs are. They're running all over the place, following the stories in their heads and their own agendas. That's what happens inside you when you're not in your Queen.

The Queen is also that part of you that has a vision for the future. Again, she's the Queen leading her Queendom, so she has a vision for the world she's creating. She plans for the future, and she's very clear on what she wants. She stays committed to that vision, taking steps forward no matter what. All the while she balances that drive with kindness and respect.

Again, men fall in love with the Queen because they can love and respect her.

The Warrioress

The Warrioress is the part of you that's a hard worker. She just gets things done. The problem is she would work herself to death.

She's pure execution, and she doesn't even care what level of priority things are at. She's happy doing laundry or buying groceries as much as she is writing executive contracts and giving speaking gigs. She's a much more primitive part of you that builds the structure for survival.

When you're in your Warrioress, you're checking things off your list: caring for the children, taking care of business, paying the bills, and cleaning the house. She's the part of you that manages your career, money, and purpose. All of the things that your Queen says she wants, the Warrioress makes happen.

But if you're too much in your Warrioress, you can lose your femininity, which means you won't attract masculine men. You may, in fact, attract a more feminine man.

So, ask yourself, *How sexy is a Warrioress helmet?* We're very serious: We want you to visualize having a helmet on every time you go into your Warrioress.

When you're in business mode, that helmet is fine. The Warrioress is particularly useful in your career. When you're working, getting things done, and making money, be the Warrioress as much as you want.

But when you're in your romantic life, set that Warrioress aside. When you're on a date or in a relationship, take off that Warrioress helmet and put on the Little Girl dress, the Lover's robe or the Queen's crown so you can be in your feminine.

The Lover

Think of Aphrodite or Cleopatra. Can you see them lounging around in beautiful surroundings (think lots of satin pillows) and enjoying themselves? That's because the Lover is all about slowing down and experiencing all her senses, slowly.

Yes, that's right. We want to hear the seduction in your voice as you talk or walk slowly and connect with your sensuality. Being sensual is all about how you talk, how you walk, what you taste, and what you smell.

The Lover is intimately connected to all five of your senses. For example, have a piece of chocolate. Rub it on your lips, smell it, and touch it. Wait some time before you take your first taste. That's being in your Lover. (At our wedding, we had a chocolate meditation where we gave everyone there a piece of chocolate and had them spend ten minutes slowly looking at it, tasting it, and enjoying it.)

Connecting with your senses expands your ability to be in anticipation—to realize that things don't have to happen right this second. It's so good to live in the unknown and connect with your Lover, who's living in the senses of right now. When you stop to enjoy the roses, your life slows down. You can watch and examine your thoughts.

A good way to think of the lover is to picture Marilyn Monroe. Step into that energy by doing things that get you into your body and your senses and allow you to experience pleasure: Get a massage, take a bubble bath, drink some champagne, have delicious food, go on a walk in nature, smell beautiful scents, look at all the beautiful colors, go to the beach, swim, and listen to beautiful music.

Sensuality and sexuality, of course, are a big part of the Lover. Be in touch with that part of yourself, which may have been closed off due to past trauma, sexual abuse, or just too much focus on structure or work (being in the masculine).

Tapping into the energy of the Lover means being more into your senses and body. Develop a connection with yourself, your hips, and your sexual organs. Even masturbation can help you get in touch with your own body, sensuality, and sexuality.

When you're the Lover, you're going to draw men to you on a primitive, sexual, and sensual level, and that's definitely a huge part of what goes into the chemistry and attraction mix.

You're going to magnetize a man, so dress beautifully and even a little sexier. Accentuate your hips and body. Be and feel sexy. Turn yourself on when you see yourself in the mirror.

This is how you draw men to you and inspire them open up to their own Lover. They'll want to just let go of work and cares, and be in pleasure with you for a while.

Seduce a man by drawing him in. He'll fall in love because of that intimate connection he can develop with you.

The Priestess

The Priestess is the part of you that's most interested in evolving your personal growth and expansion. If something traumatic happens—a divorce, for example—we call it a Priestess moment because she wakes you up to the truth of who you really are.

She's fierce and unapologetic, and she'll do whatever it takes to bring you back into your power. If you've given all your power away and then become angry, that anger is your Priestess saying, "Enough is enough."

Your Priestess is that part of you that solves problems and figures things out. She's creative and artistic, and she finds ways to break through your barriers. She helps you get over your internal demons, struggles, and limiting beliefs.

The Priestess is about the truth of the situation, of what you want, and of the solution. She doesn't take any lies or B.S. from yourself or anyone else. She's a wise woman. You might also think of her as a shaman, a fairy godmother, or the good witch from *The Wizard of Oz*. She gets things ready, puts you on the right path, and helps you figure out what your next steps are.

When you say, "I can't live like this anymore. I can't live to just the status quo. I can't just dim my light anymore," that's your Priestess talking. She's all about helping you shine your light and be fully self-expressed—to be in that unapologetically, consistently, fully grounded state from the highest to the lowest dimensions. When you're in your Priestess, you're fully integrated.

On a scale of 1 to 10, how does your Priestess do at being a problem-solver; being creative; standing in your truth; overcoming your old issues, limiting beliefs, and fears; and standing for what you really want and the way you were meant to be? How does she do at holding other people to that as well?

Being well-read and educated is also part of the Priestess. Work on yourself and stay up-to-date with things in the world. That intellectual and creative development stimulates a man on that level as well.

This important energy inspires men to develop an intellectual and creative connection with you.

The Little Girl

There's a part inside you that's still a child. She may like bright colors, flowers, and arts and crafts, and she likes to be creative.

She may be very spontaneous and live in the moment. This is your Little Girl energy.

The Little Girl forgets where she is and who is around her, so she's able to surrender in that very moment. She's also good at being innovative. She explores other ways of understanding or seeing things. She can discover ways to label an object as something completely new.

The Little Girl is important to your romantic life. You need to fully embrace this energy because this is the part of you that men really fall in love with—this playful, curious, fun, feminine energy that's like a little girl on the playground. She has fun jumping around, playing, dancing, singing, and twirling. That's the Little Girl energy that brings out a man's protective instinct.

Where would you rank yourself right now on a scale of 1 to 10 for the Little Girl archetype? How in touch are you with it? How frequently do you express it?

Try to step into this energy more. It could be helpful to buy some props, such as a frilly dress, for expressing your Little Girl archetype.

You may be thinking, *I'm not that spontaneous. I'm more reserved. I'm more reasonable. I didn't grow up like that.* Go back into your childhood and think about something that you really liked to do when you were little. Maybe it was music or playing a certain instrument. Maybe it was simply swinging on the playground or playing in the sand.

The Little Girl isn't logical and she doesn't take every label as a given. She asks, "Wait, is this painting really a painting or can I wear it like a cape?" She challenges everything and everyone's worldview.

She has imaginary friends. Her imaginary faculty, her right brain, is very strongly developed. She's creative, playful, and curious.

What blocks keep you from stepping into the Little Girl? What negative labels do you put on her? One common label is "immature." And she absolutely is! The Little Girl is totally immature. That's her gift!

What keeps you from stepping into the Little Girl? You may think something like, *Whenever I'm in the Little Girl, I get betrayed and taken advantage of.*

First of all, how do you know that? How do you know these things happened because you were in the Little Girl? We often wrongly assume a connection when there's merely a correlation. Keep in mind that there are many variables that contribute to whatever phenomenon or thoughts you experience.

Secondly, what is your relationship with your own inner girl? Because if you don't embrace your her, nobody else will. It's that simple. You attract who you're being. We live in a mirroring universe, so the more you love yourself, the more the world will love you.

Antia's friends really appreciate her being in her Little Girl because she obviously loves her inner girl. She did the happy hippo dance in the middle of the room at her own birthday party, not caring if anyone saw.

Finally, when you're in touch with your own Little Girl and take care of that relationship with her, she won't sabotage you. Instead, she'll behave well during important moments.

The Wild Woman

The Wild Woman is that part of you that's totally free and uninhibited. She doesn't care about rules or what anyone else thinks. She just does what she wants to and doesn't really give a hoot. In a way, she's just crazy.

She's that part of you that's purely instinctual, like an animal. She has the killer, mating, and eating instinct.

Sometimes Antia even calls her the Murderess. By whichever name, she's that part of you that says, "I don't care. This is what needs to happen, and this is what I want to do," then goes for it. No restraints, no rules, no restrictions.

The Wild Woman sets you free because her primitive nature knows no boundaries. Her brain isn't well developed, nor did it need to be when she originated. The world she came from wasn't as complex as today's world. And although that primitive nature means you need to integrate her into society, she's actually the most grounded, best rooted part of you.

It's really important to embrace her. If you don't, you'll feel the anger and other emotions brewing inside you because she wants to be expressed.

You know you're lacking the energy of the Wild Woman if you've struggled with setting boundaries, been afraid to step on people's toes, didn't want to be disliked, avoided hurting other people's feelings, or wanted to be polite and nice.

The Wild Woman is more like the Bitch from Chapter 2 who says "I don't care what anyone else thinks about me. This is what I want. I'm going to do this for me." She's more like an animal in that animals don't go around wondering if it's polite to grab a piece of meat from the kill. No, animals just go for it.

This energy is so attractive to men. The Wild Woman in you can help your man break free of his own restraints and worries about what people think. By following your example, he can fully express who he really is.

The Wild Woman is your support because she has so much power and isn't reasonable. Sometimes, when you allow yourself to be raw and real, the most bizarre experiences come to you. For example, you push your boundaries in sex by just doing something different. The Wild Woman can bring a lot of variety into your life.

She's also that part of you that holds anger and knows how to express it. If you've had a hard time letting out your anger, you might just practice throwing a Wild Woman temper tantrum to let it all out. Scream into your pillow while kicking your legs into your mattress. Anger is powerful and can be transformative and useful if, like a Wild Woman, you know how to set it free.

No Doormat is connected to her Wild Woman. When you're fully connected to your Wild Woman, you get respect and you may even be slightly intimidating. Don't worry though—a dose of Wild Woman can be just right when balanced with the other archetypes.

You'll be intimidating to men who aren't in touch with their Wild Man, but men who are will see you as their playmate. So even if you're totally polished, you've got to let it rip somewhere. Otherwise, your inner Wild Woman, who doesn't care about things like your Ph.D. or the five languages you speak, will sabotage you.

Remember: All your archetypes need to have a place in your life.

So rank yourself on a scale of 1 to 10 for how in touch you are with your Wild Woman. See where you're strong and where you may need more help with that energy.

Homeplay: Strengthen Your Archetypes

Review where you ranked yourself with the archetypes. You may need to start doing some activities and exercises to get into all the parts.

Weak in the Queen? Create a vision for yourself. Write down your five-year plan. What do you really want? Create a list, put it on your wall and stay committed to it. Think about getting a crown. Put yourself in balance, treat yourself like a queen, and respect yourself.

Weak in the Warrioress? Put together a to-do list and take action. Identify stuff that you've been putting off, then get it done.

Weak in the Lover? Put on some sensual music. Run a bubble bath and have some champagne, play some beautiful music and light beautifully scented candles. Get a massage or take part in another kind of sensual activity.

Weak in the Priestess? Read a self-improvement book, meditate, or pray. Maybe do some incantations and trust that the energy is moving through you. If you feel drawn to speak at an event, just ding the glass and do a speech. You're even exercising your Priestess by reading this book and learning. Get a Tarot or angel card reading, or take a personality test. All of these things can help get you into the intellectual Priestess energy.

Weak in the Little Girl? Go to the playground. Hang out and do something playful. Wear a frilly dress, dance to some music, or get some crayons and draw. Do something that helps you to get into the Little Girl energy.

Weak in the Wild Woman? Throw a temper tantrum! Scream into a pillow, or do an ecstatic dance or anything that's really animalistic. Watch some nature documentaries or go to the zoo and watch the animals. Go out in nature and just let yourself be free. Run around and roam like a Wild Woman.

Start taking action. Become familiar with and connect to all of the archetypes within you. Again, when you're in balance, you're going to be the most magnetic to your ideal man.

If you have any questions or would like some help connecting to your archetypes, book a complimentary 1:1 "Magnetize Your Man" Fifteen-Minute Dating Clarity with Antia at MagnetizeYourMan.com.

We would love to support you, help you to discover yourself, and answer any questions you have on where you may be blocked. We hope to help you find balance, be your most magnetic self, and have your magnificent man in your life very soon.

We're so excited for you to start stepping into your full power and magnetism!

Chapter 6: How & Where To Meet High-Quality Men

It's important to attract a quality man into your life. Let's go deeper into the secrets of how to meet one. In short, we'll teach you the art of attracting HIM.

On the one hand, this sounds so simple, right? You're a socially confident woman who knows how to move around in the dating world.

Or are you?

In her dating journey, Antia didn't know how to connect to a man who was aligned with her on all levels. She met men who were spiritually aligned and maybe even physically connected but who lacked a mental/intellectual connection with her. She met men she was very intellectually compatible with but who offered no chemistry or spiritual alignment.

In order to get yourself more into the right man's energy field, you have to determine where the quality man is coming from and what his approach is. Knowing this will help you determine what sort of man he really is.

For instance, a quality man isn't looking for a woman, he's actually focusing on his purpose. Brody knows this well because he's on his mission. He has what is best called *drive*. You won't find him in the bars because the men in bars are usually looking for someone to fill an emptiness in their life. The quality men you're seeking are usually busy traveling the world, attending charity events, and making a big difference in the world. They're passionate about the world, their career, their life, and giving back.

So how do you find them?

Go where they go: High-quality men are most likely working on themselves, so look for them in self-development workshops. These men will be focused on anything that's about business, even about growing their finances, because they're very conscious about everything in their life: Self-improvement, food, nutrition, and health are topics that capture their attention.

Do what you love! Start engaging with activities, hobbies, classes, workshops, events, groups, and places you enjoy. Find where those two areas intersect—what you love and where there's potential to meet high-quality men!

Make a list of the activities, interests, groups, and passions you've ever been interested in or curious about. Think dancing, pottery, sports, workshops, seminars, a spiritual practice, self-improvement, political activism, pet groups, vegan groups, scuba diving, sailing, surfing—there are so many different areas.

Here's a list of some more:

Hiking groups and events
Dance groups and events
Singles groups and events
Workshops, classes, talks and seminars
Speed dating groups and events
Self-improvement groups and events
Discussion and support groups
Networking and business networking groups and events
Volunteering and charity groups and events
Religious and spiritual groups and events
Political groups and events

Co-ed sports and exercise groups and events
Music groups and events
Special interest groups and events
Improv and comedy groups and events
Acting groups and events
Toastmasters groups and events
Yoga groups and events
Book groups and events
Cooking groups and events
Foodie groups and events
Meditation groups and events
Fitness groups and events
Speaking groups and events
Social groups and events
International groups and events
Law of Attraction groups and events
Business, money, and investing groups and events
Technology groups and events
BNI (Business Networking International) groups and events
Entrepreneur groups and events
Referral networking groups and events
Age-specific groups and events
Boardgames groups and events
Online marketing groups and events
Real estate groups and events
Grand openings
Art galleries and art shows

Make Meeting People and Having Fun Your Priority

Complete your list and circle the activities that are both social and filled with opportunities to meet people.

The part about meeting people is crucial. For example, a comedy nightclub would be great fun but not an ideal way to meet someone. Comedy clubs are a destination where the crowd is focused on the act, then leave when the act is over. There's no opportunity to mingle.

So find places, events, and activities that will allow you to socialize. This is why classes, workshops, activities, and hiking are optimal. Search for great groups and events to be a part of or potentially join. We recommend joining a group and going to the first meeting for at least fifteen to thirty minutes to give it a real chance. If you're not feeling it, you can always go home or try another group or event.

But always keep in mind that you'll meet a quality man by being a quality woman.

Remember: Fate Comes in Many Forms

As you meet new people, don't jump to conclusions about anyone. If you find yourself talking to a new person and saying to yourself, *He's not my type*, quiet that inner voice. The man you're talking to at, say, a foreign language class, may not be the man you desire. But he could end up introducing you to your man! So stay open and talk to people.

You could also step into the role of a "connector." Always look for an opportunity to connect a man who's not right for you with a girlfriend he might be a good match for. Don't think only about yourself. After all, what goes around comes around.

Antia had a situation a few years before she met Brody. She met a really great guy—good-looking, successful, accomplished—but they didn't have chemistry and didn't really connect. So, she introduced him to one of her girlfriends, and the two of them started dating. So, you never know why you're meeting that man.

Focus on the Fun, not the Outcome

Just have fun! When you're in a fun energy and enjoying yourself, it's going to make it much more likely that you'll leave your house and go out.

Why? Because if you're doing something you enjoy and look forward to, you're more likely to show up in the first place. We love that quote from Woody Allen: "Eighty percent of success is showing up." You've got to show up, and that's going to help you overcome that inner critical voice.

Also, it's important to go into these situations unattached to the outcome. Be committed only to having fun and enjoying yourself—don't be tied to the expectation that you'll meet the man of your dreams. That's because, ironically, going into these situations with no expectations for anything but fun makes you more appealing and easier to approach. And that may lead you to your man.

Here's the recipe for not being attached to the outcome: Don't get lost in asking yourself:

Is he the one?
Where's this going?
Should I get his number?
I hope he asks me on a date.

The more fun you have, the easier it is to let go of the outcome and just be present. We know it's counterintuitive, but we also know it's true: When you live in the moment without anticipations about the future, the future can approach you.

So stop thinking about the future and the past and letting fears overtake you. Living in the now will bring the men to you like honeybees to a rose.

If you stay in your zone and enjoy your life, you'll find that life delivers surprises. Antia actually met a man in traffic once.

They were driving parallel to each other, and as the L.A. traffic crawled along, he signaled to her to roll down her window, and they exchanged phone numbers. She certainly wasn't looking for a man to hand her a phone number that day. She was focused on other things and being in her zone—and it just happened. And that sort of thing could happen to you if you let it.

Life has many surprises in store for you when you're open to it.

Online Dating

Yes, online dating can be another option. But don't focus only on it. You want to create multiple streams of meeting men. We recommend treating the next one to three months like a fun research project, like you're a love alchemist creating and running your new "love laboratory!"

If you decide to use online dating as one stream, get a great photo of yourself and write a short paragraph about your ideal life and ideal relationship. Provide an appetizer of what that looks like so a man can put himself into that picture and think to himself, *You know what? That's what I really want too. That sounds amazing.* He may reach out to you and discover areas that are unique about you and want to connect with those as well.

Try sites like OkCupid, Match, Plenty of Fish (POF), Millionaire Match, or even Hinge or Tinder. Just put your profile out like bait. You're fishing rather than hunting. Show up, put out the bait, and let the man come to you.

Make sure your profile contains only classy photos. Look squarely into the camera and don't wear sunglasses. Don't be three hundred feet away from the camera, but also don't be too close.

And make sure that at least one photo is at least from the waist up. Feel free to share a full-body shot. Don't worry if you have a few more pounds and you're curvier—it's beautiful! A lot of men love that, so show it off. Be proud of your body and be confident. Otherwise, you project a repelling, hidden energy—and that never works.

Keep your bio light, sweet, and focused on the best things about you. You want to give men just a peek to intrigue them and inspire them to want to learn more. Don't stuff them so full of information right up front that they think they already know everything about you. You want to create a little bit of desire, a little mystery, a little intrigue. More on that in Chapters 8 and 9.

Put up your profile and let men message you. Peruse the messages occasionally, maybe once or twice a week, and see which ones you're interested in. Don't put a lot of energy or time into it. Think of online dating sites as just one option—not your only option. You really never know if your man is going to come through an online dating message, a friend, a colleague, church, or a group.

Other Online Options

You can meet men on online sites other than dating sites!

Antia met Brody at a spiritual/self-improvement discussion Meetup group from Meetup.com, which is one of our favorite websites. In fact, we feel it's the best website for finding these kinds of groups and events.

Meetup.com includes different groups of people in your area with varying hobbies or interests. It provides an avenue for people to gather, share their interests, and take part in activities and events.

Go to Meetup.com and do a search. You can either use keywords to find relevant groups, or just browse all the different groups in your area. Look for groups that match your favorite interests and activities. Join any that look interesting.

You can also browse Facebook.com/Discover or Eventbrite.com to see upcoming events Lastly, you can use Google to search for interests or event calendars in your area.

Follow Your Inspiration!

Don't just push yourself to go from one event to the next. Find your best sources and follow your gut. When Antia met Brody, she'd had a nudge that she listened to. Something told her that she just had to go to Meetup and find a group. It was an intuitive hit.

Don't go to event sites with a logical mindset. Why? Because women are always in one of four different chemical and hormonal states every month, so almost every week feels different. Some weeks you'll move forward quickly and with a lot of intensity and passion, and other weeks your body invites you to retreat, learn about yourself, maybe read a little more, stay home, and trust the ebb and flow of life.

But, we do recommend that you go out at least once a week to a social event or activity. Meeting people will feed that energy of abundance within you. You'll begin to be aware that you have options. You'll start feeling more social and, most importantly, start having fun!

Make Events Your Valuable Tool

However often you get out, aim to be consistent. Make it a regular practice to get out there and be open and available for the right man to come to you.

If you spend all your time at work or home, you won't be available for a man to approach you. In the real world, Mr. Right won't just show up on your doorstep with a ring and a marriage proposal. You have to make the effort to be available.

It's all about being aware of yourself, tracking your actions, and trying to discover how you subconsciously work. For that reason, we encourage you to design your own Dating Tracking Sheet. Keep track of:

What you liked about an event or date
What could be improved on
What was missing
What your internal dialogue was like

You'll learn so much about yourself by keeping track of these details. For example, do you go into every event with the same attitude and mindset? Do you ever realize that you feel better after one kind of even than another? This Tracker Sheet will help you discover aspects about yourself that will be useful over time and valuable overall.

Success is all about distinctions. You're not just doing this blindly and floating around. Live by design, not default.

How to Prepare for an Event

No matter what kind of event it is, dress in a way that makes you feel attractive. Dress how a queen would dress—feel attractive and sexy, like you're a prize.

How you dress is directly proportional to how you feel on the inside. The same goes for your makeup and hair. Even if you're just going out to a basic event, make sure you feel good about how you look because the better you feel about yourself, the more attractive you are to others.

Before you leave the house, put on some fun music that makes you feel sexy, attractive, fun, and happy. Dance while you're putting on your makeup, curling your hair, or getting dressed! It's going to get you in a positive and happy state. And keep it going on your way there. This is important because when you're in a positive, happy state, you're going to be more likely to smile, be open, and give off the vibe that you're available. You're going to radiate an attractive energy draws more men to you.

To help boost your energy and give off a Queenly vibe, give yourself positive affirmations, such as:

I love myself.
I'm awesome.
I'm sexy.
Men love me.
I'm a catch.
Any man would be lucky to be with me.
I'm a Queen.
I'm the prize.
My life is awesome.
I'm great. I'm always moving forward.
I'm always moving to the next level.

Carefully select any of these positive thoughts or create your own—whatever resonates for you and makes you feel great.

Professional athletes and astronauts do this mental pre-rehearsal. When the mind imagines something, it doesn't know the difference between imagination and reality. This means your mind is seeing it actually happening, is preparing for it, and starts to create it as reality. If you believe that you had an incredible experience, at some point you actually will.

How to Make the Most of Your Events

There are some interesting additional key components here that are really powerful. Most people reach their peak social state after at least three interactions. So, when you've talked to at least three people, you're in your best social energy and are your best social self.

To use this principle at your next event, say hello to the doorman, the host, or any staff you encounter right off the bat. If food is being served, greet a server. Say hello to the bartender if there is one. Say hello to somebody you're standing next to in line. You can open up the dialogue with a general question like:

How's your day/evening going so far?
What brings you to this event?
How long have you been living here in [fill in name of city]?
Where are you from originally?
What do you most love to do for fun around here?
Do you have any fun plans for the weekend?
Do you like to travel? Where to?

Remember to smile. Set aside thoughts about work, your kids, your family or ex, and everything in the past. Just focus on your present. Smiling when you're out is very attractive. In fact, it's magnetic and draws men to you. Eighty percent of your communication is nonverbal. So your body language says a lot!

Many women have closed body language when they're out. Or they talk to and face only their friends. Their body language says, *I'm focusing on this person and this person only. Don't bother me.* Men don't approach them because they're reading that body language. And later, the women complain that men never approach them!

You want to send the opposite message. You want to communicate that you're open and would welcome someone's approach. Stand so that you have open shoulders (as opposed to being hunched over), an open smile (instead of an anxious frown), and arms that are relaxed at your sides (not crossed over your chest). Be your radiant Queen so that men can feel like a King when they come up to you.

You may not believe this, but the biggest fear most men have is rejection. They won't approach you if they feel there's a chance that you'll reject them. Closed-off body language definitely suggests that chance. So make sure you don't have the so-called "resting bitch face." This is why it's so important to feel good when you're at these events. Have a good time and enjoy yourself. Smile, be open, be social, and show the world—and men—that you're talkative, eager to meet people, receptive, and approachable. This radiant energy will attract a man to you.

Once a man does come up to you, you can choose to have a conversation or not. You don't have to talk to a man for very long; you can excuse yourself, but praise yourself for being open and available! Eventually, the man who approaches you will be the right one.

If there's a certain man you're interested in, you want to make it as easy as possible for him to approach. Stand next to him to make it convenient for him to talk to you. It's much easier for a man to just turn and say, "Hello, how's your night going?" than to walk all the way across the room through a wall of people to talk to you.

Finally, many women feel safer going to events or activities with friends. Keep in mind that when you're out with friends, you don't want to have a closed circle. Open that group up and allow a man into your space. Or leave your group of friends briefly to make yourself available to a man who has had his eye on you. Wander over to explore the bar, get food by yourself, go for a slow walk to the restroom. Give a man the opportunity to approach you.

Advice for Introverts

If you're introverted, you may need to go into the bathroom, look in the mirror and anchor the word *trust* or *courage* by repeating those words silently to yourself a few times when you're out.

You always have to make sure you're centered because introverts are easily swayed by other people's energy. If this is you, you have to learn to bring attention and focus back to yourself. You can ask yourself questions regularly, such as *Can I feel my feet on the ground? Can I feel my butt in the chair?*

Make sure you're always in your body. Many women actually energetically leave their body the minute they go walk out of their home or sit down for a date or an event because it feels uncomfortable.

Also, make sure that you keep breathing. You'd be surprised to learn how often you may be holding your breath when you're out. Why is that? Well, being out in a group of people is an uncomfortable zone for you, so you go into survival mode. Subconsciously, you don't know if you'll need to run, so you hold your breath.

It helps to take breaks in the bathroom for some deep breaths. Repeat to yourself that, *I trust. I'm open.* Having a few little anchors like that will help you. It doesn't have to be much—just enough to recalibrate your system.

How to Talk to Someone You Just Met

One valuable aspect about communication is that people love to talk about themselves. So, the great thing you can do is just ask a man questions and let him do most of the talking.

You can keep him going with just, "That's interesting. Wow, tell me more." The more he talks, the more he starts to feel invested in the conversation, and the more he starts to feel invested in you.

This isn't necessarily a man/woman type of thing. This works for all interactions. If you really want someone to feel invested in you and to like you quickly, let them talk about themselves.

If you're worried about being bored, ask a man about things you're actually interested in (whether that's the topic he's on or himself in general). By answering your questions, he gets to prove himself to you. He'll start to feel like you're a woman who actually cares and is interested in him. This will make him feel flattered and want to spend more time with you.

However, pay attention to see if he asks you questions. Even if you end up asking the majority of the questions, you'll want to know if he seems willing to inquire about you. If you want him to ask you more about yourself, simply stop talking and smile. The uncomfortable silence will compel him to ask you something.

And what if you find yourself talking to someone you don't want to keep talking to? Just take one step backward and say, "I really enjoyed our visit. Have a wonderful rest of your evening." Say it with a smile and then leave.

Always Keep Your Options Open

Lastly, even if you meet a man you're interested in, you should still date other men. Why? Because it will create an energy of abundance in your life. You don't want to act out of a sense of scarcity and focus on just one man.

We call this *one-itis*, where you focus on one man and see him as your only possibility. Instead, make sure you're living a life of abundance. Make sure you have multiple options.

You're going to find the right man. And when you do, make sure you're creating the energy that makes him see you as the prize you are. Make him see you as a woman many other men would be happy to be with. And when you choose him, he'll be thrilled. That's why it's so important to meet and date multiple men. Even if there's a gentleman you're really interested in, you still want to go out and meet other quality men, if for nothing else, to build or grow a great social life.

Homeplay: Get out There and Start Meeting People!

Go to at least one event a week. Become curious about yourself. You might even want to journal what your approach was before this homeplay and how it changes. Note events you attend and your feelings about what you thought the outcome would be. Jot down any thoughts you had, such as, *I'll never meet someone anyway* or *I hope they don't notice that I'm shy.* Ask yourself what you could say to yourself next time instead. Write everything out for yourself and become the researcher.

If you don't already have an online dating profile, put some together. Give OkCupid, Plenty of Fish (POF) and Match a try. Use nice, classy photos and let the profiles sit there for a while—just see what happens.

Go out and practice the tips this chapter covers.

We'd love to hear about your experiences and answer your questions in our Magnetize Your Man Free Private Facebook group,. You can find it at

https://MagnetizeYourMan.com/FreeGroup or by searching "Magnetize Your Man" on Facebook.

Remember, having a fun and interesting life will make dating fun and lead you to meeting men who are worth your time. The key is taking consistent action and working through any resistance that comes up.

You can do this!

Chapter 7: Captivating Communication

In this chapter we go deeper into techniques and strategies that can help you effectively communicate and connect with men so that they can be even more attracted and interested in you. Also, these tips will help you have a loving, long-term relationship in which you can connect and share your heart in a powerful way—and help a man open up and share his heart as well.

This topic is near and dear to our hearts. When Antia was going on her countless first dates (few led to a second date), she made every mistake possible. She was so empathetic with the men that she often developed a psychologist/patient dynamic with them. It was a safe way for her to avoid making herself vulnerable. Instead, men opened up and told her all their deepest, darkest secrets. But since this communication had a dynamic of hierarchy and the topics went so deep so fast, the men had no choice but to run for the hills afterwards.

Having captivating communication means you're able to communicate with a man in a way that allows each of you to feel understood. It allows you to have a smooth interaction that will end with him being more interested and attracted to you. He'll feel lucky to have you in his life and want to be in a long-term relationship with you.

Being an effective communicator will also make you stand out. All the men in a room will gravitate to you and wonder who you are. They'll know there's something special about you and want to know you more.

Captivating communication is also the key ingredient for keeping a man. It's one thing to magnetize him, but it's another to keep him intrigued and interested enough to keep asking you out.

When you go to a social event, focus on having a communication style that draws a man to you and feeds his interest in you. (Secret: You don't really have to do a lot of work.)

Let's start with who should do the talking, and when and why.

Talking vs. Listening

There are two types of women: The talker and the listener.

Which one are you? If you're a talker and haven't had success with it, it may be because:

You're connecting and speaking from a place of nervousness or fear.

You use speaking to avoid feeling and being in the moment.

You're talking so much that it turns into you selling yourself to him instead of him selling himself to you.

If this happens to you, here's how to change it: Switch it up. Invite him to share some of his experiences out of genuine interest. After you're done sharing something, simply ask, "And you?"

The paradox here is that the way to be a captivating communicator with a man is, ironically, to let him do most of the talking.

You don't have to do a lot of work to have a great conversation with a man. Just be present. Feel good, feel attractive, feel like the Queen. Relax, allow, and ask intriguing questions. Let him sell himself to you and show you how great he is, because when he's talking about himself and proving himself to you, he starts to feel like he's investing more in you.

There's a direct correlation here. The more he talks to you and the more you listen, the more he sells himself, and the more he starts to like you.

Here, you might think to yourself, *He doesn't like me at all because he doesn't know anything about me. He just likes the way he feels when he's bragging about himself.* Again, use this technique only if you've been the talker in the past and it hasn't worked for you.

If you're primarily a listener and it hasn't worked for you, it may be because:

You're focusing exclusively on him with no regard for yourself.

He feels like you're closed off or don't like him.

In some cases, you can also run the risk of the interaction turning into a patient/counselor dynamic in which he makes himself so vulnerable that it doesn't feel safe to him to ask you out on a second date.

Keeping it Light to Start

When Antia started dating, it took her some time to learn that she had to keep it light. As a matter of fact, she had many first dates that never went to a second date for this exact reason. She always went really deep right away, and it was just a little too much, too fast.

This kind of oversharing can lead to the man thinking, *This is a little too much. I'm just getting to know her and now she's giving me her whole life story and her deepest fears.* Or, it could be the other way around: *I gave her too much of my life story and deepest fears.*

Either scenario rarely leads to a second date. So it's generally best to stick with fun and light topics in the beginning.

Here are some great questions that you can ask on a first date:

If you were an animal, what would you be?

If you were a kitchen utensil, which would you be and why?

You might be thinking, *Seriously?* Yes. As a matter of fact, we're serious. Antia learned from her own experience how useful and fun these questions can be. Have fun with it. Just enjoy yourself, because it's infectious.

Or, use escape (or fun) topics. Most people are bored, don't really like their jobs, or are possibly even slightly depressed. This is statistically the case in most countries. So, avoid boring and depressing topics on early dates.

It's a bit risky to go deeper into what a man does for work right away unless you know that he loves his job. People also generally don't feel great talking about their problems and frustrations. They also don't want to talk about the weather or boring aspects of life, so keep to fun topics.

How to Be Captivating

Great questions and topics can make for great conversations.

Go to Facebook and look at some of the best questions that people post on their profiles. Write down the ones you like and become the best question-asker ever!

It almost doesn't matter what he answers, but you get a crown for just asking a creative question. So many people are used to the usual questions (What do you do? What are your hobbies? Where are you from?) So try to ask something different such as:

What are you not passionate about?
What don't you do for work?
What's your favorite childhood memory?
What was your favorite toy?

Just pick a topic that most people don't think about. An unexpected question can be fun for him to answer and help you learn something about him. It also creates an early connection that's a great place for a relationship to start.

Balancing the Conversation

If you feel like he's not letting you do any talking, realize that communication is a balancing act. Learn to lean back energetically and allow his energy to come to you, too. You want a man who's just as interested in you and isn't an egocentric who likes to talk only about himself.

If you begin to feel like he's dominating the conversation, it's fine to force the balance yourself. Just pause after he's finished talking and smile. He'll feel the gap and the tension of that little bit of awkward silence. This should motivate him to ask a question about you. People tend to want to ask you the same questions that you asked them, so be prepared to answer some of those great questions you just served up. Remember to keep it fun and light.

The Importance of Conversing Without Chasing

When you're socializing, don't chase men. That's why we recommend no initiating anything with a man romantically. You can still initiate the conversation when you're out as long as you're just being social and having fun. But, remember to avoid hitting on a guy or trying too hard to get him interested in you.

Your only goal should be being social, having fun, and letting go of the outcome. As long as you do that, you'll be in your Queen energy and in your best state. Whatever happens, let it happen. Just be present in the moment and enjoy yourself!

Stay Grounded

When you're talking to a man, make sure that you stay in your body. So many women don't focus on themselves or stay in their bodies in conversation. When that happens it's because a woman feels uncomfortable and awkward.

To remain focused, feel your feet on the ground. If you're sitting, ask yourself, *Do I feel my butt on this chair? Do I feel the back of the chair*? If the answer is no, remind yourself to stay present and in your body.

It's so important to stay in the moment and in the conversation—to be present and not floating around inside your head. The man can tell if you've checked out. Make sure that both of your feet are firmly flat on the ground—not pulled back with your toes hanging—especially if you tend to get nervous in conversations. Keeping your feet on the ground will stabilize you energetically.

The Mindset of Captivating Communication

In general, when you're having conversations with men, most of what you're communicating is non-verbal. Studies have shown that that 80 to 90 percent of what you're communicating isn't even with your words. It's with your body and your energy.

That's why how you prepare before you go out and how you're feeling when you're out are so important. Men will pick up on things you don't say. So make sure you feel good, have fun, enjoy yourself, and let go of any attachment to the outcome. This puts you in your best and most attractive state.

Commit to being present. Enjoy the journey and the process, and put your energy into showing up and being the best you can be. Just enjoy socializing and having the best conversations. Let go of caring whether he asks you out, if you'll get a second date, if he wants to take things further or even if he likes you.

Also, tell yourself positive thoughts before you leave home and while you're out:

> I'm a Queen!
> I'm the most attractive woman and any man would be lucky to be with me!
> I'm a catch!
> I'm the prize!
> I love myself!
> I'm beautiful!
> I'm worthy!
> I'm amazing!
> I deserve to have exactly what I want in life!

This will draw him to you and captivate him. If it's clear to him that you're happy, fulfilled, and enjoying life, he's going to see you as a lot more mysterious. He'll be curious about you and will want to know what fuels your joy.

You always want to create a little bit of mystery. You don't want to lay everything on the table right away. Don't be blatant or too upfront, telling him over the first coffee date the whole history of your past relationships and everything that's happened in your life. You want him to be a little bit curious so he's challenged to solve you like a puzzle.

Be the dancer who reveals only a little bit of herself as she twirls, mostly hidden by a silky scarf. Reveal only enough to interest him—but not everything at once. Give him just enough to make him continue thinking about you after the date ends.

Also, don't forget to breathe. Really, so many women in conversations don't breathe enough. Breathing intentionally is a great way to connect with yourself and reassure yourself that you're safe.

When you're out, in addition to positive mental affirmations, you can also set up little reminders or notes for yourself on your phone or put them in your wallet. Peek at them when you're in the bathroom or by yourself for a moment. They can be things like:

Am I grounded?
Do I feel my feet?
Do I feel confident?
I'm the queen.
I'm powerful.
I'm sexy.
I'm a catch.

These little reminders will help you get back on track if you start feeling insecure.

Also, it's so important to respond to him appropriately and be aware of how things are progressing. Don't push or become anxious if you feel that he may be withdrawing. Let the process just naturally unfold. If he does withdraw, remember that another man is around the corner and ready to enter your life. The worst thing you can do is become anxious and start talking faster if he's obviously trying to make his way out of the conversation.

Respond and adjust to whatever happens.

Body Language

It's great to smile a lot while remaining natural. That's why we encourage you to have fun, play music, and get into a good energy place before you leave your house. These steps make it easier for you to smile, and that smile is going to come off as more attractive.

Open body language is key. Don't fold your arms or cross your legs, and don't "shrink" yourself. He'll feel that energy and sense that you're closed off—that you're not available. It will most likely cause him to close himself off in response and not be as available to you.

Whatever it is that you want him to do, be the mirror for him. So, if you want him to relax, you have to relax. Allow your arms to just fall to your side, open your chest, and allow your shoulders to gently fall back. You don't have to stand like a soldier though.

If you want him to have fun, you have to have fun. If you want him to feel confident, you have to feel confident. If you want him to feel attractive, you have to feel attractive. So, you have to go first and be the source of what you want to have more of.

Also, when you're sitting, keep your torso at a 90-degree angle to your legs, or even lean back. Some women lean forward too much and are too interested in the man, just like a little puppy. You want to lean back a little bit, like the Queen sitting on your throne. Smile and have an open body language.

If you're standing, just stand tall without leaning in too much.

Also, wear clothes that make you feel attractive and sexy. Fix your hair and everything else so that you feel attractive. All of that is going to be great for your body language.

Wrapping it Up Successfully

If you really enjoyed your time with him, make sure that you let him know this as the date winds down. Be sure to make it very specific about him. For instance, tell him that he shared something that really inspired you. It will provide an opening and a door for him to ask you out for the next date.

Again, you can start sharing more about yourself about three to six dates into the relationship. You can also start asking him more about his dating history, his family, his job, and things like that. This is when you can both begin to be vulnerable with each other.

A lot of women ask us, "How do I know if a man is just looking to sleep around? How do I know if he really wants a serious relationship or if he just wants to keep things casual?"

Our suggestion is to ask him! Here are some questions to ask him:

When it comes to dating, what are you looking for right now?
What do you want when it comes to dating?
When it comes to your romantic life, what are you looking for and what are your main goals?

Most men will share and be honest with you. Some may tell you that they just want to have fun right now or just explore. Others will tell you that they're looking for a serious, long-term relationship.

Also, actions speak louder than words. So watch his actions carefully. Judge his body language and his actions more so than his words. You learn a lot more about someone by taking in the whole picture.

Signs that he's looking for a casual relationship:

He calls at late hours.
He doesn't give you that Saturday night date.
He makes sexual advances really fast.
He never goes really deep in conversation.
He doesn't really listen to you.
He makes sexual compliments, like "You are sexy."

Signs that he's looking for a serious relationship:

He's a gentleman.
He takes his time with sexual advances.
He's interested in you.
He's available Saturday night.
He calls during the day and at night.

Navigating Conflict

One of the best ways to navigate conflict with a man is with open dialogue. This technique is basically a series of three questions. You begin by first asking him how he's feeling and what his thoughts are.

Stephen Covey, in his book *Seven Habits of Highly Effective People*, says it's important to try to understand before you seek to be understood.

Ask the following questions to learn more about where a man's at before you share what you want or need.

Question #1: "How are you feeling right now?" Or "How are you feeling right now about XYZ?"
XYZ would be whatever area that conflict is in. So you can replace that with "the relationship" or "our date" or "the conversation we just had." Just hear what he has to say and don't pay much attention to the story. Mostly observe the emotion.

Question #2: "Why are you feeling that way?"
If he mentioned any emotions in his first answer (especially negative ones), ask him about those. For example, if he said he was feeling frustrated, ask him why. You want to actually ask him so you're very clear on why he thinks he's feeling that way instead of why you think he's feeling that way. Again, just listen and let him express.

Question #3: "What do you want?"
This question is especially helpful if you want a really good way to understand fully where he's coming from and what he's wanting. For example, you can ask something such as, "And what do you want right now with that?" or "And how would you most like that to be different or improve?"

Ask the questions and let him respond. Listen and be present without taking things personally or as criticisms. Try to be curious and open.

After he's shared and you've fully listened and sought to understand him fully, then you can share your side of things in the framework of those same three questions. He'll be much more receptive to what you have to share. Often, he'll even return the questions himself after you've asked them. But if not, it's your turn.

Once you've shared your emotions and point of view and he's had the chance to understand where you're coming from, you can understand each other more as the relationship progresses. You'll be better able to get on the same page as a team and look for and negotiate solutions.

Always ask, "How can we adjust things as needed so that we can both be fully happy? What could be a win/win solution for us both?"

You can navigate almost anything, whether it's how often you see each other, who will pay for dinner, who does the dishes when, or whatever else might come up in conflicts two people may have.

It could be something that you're uncomfortable with or something he might be acting strange about. You need to get clarity and understanding so that you can connect and get on the same page with each other.

The Acknowledgement Sandwich

We highly recommend that early on, even on your first date, you speak up right away if you notice something that bothers you or that may help him understand your wants and needs better. That way, you communicate clearly to him. If you mention it later, he may say, "Why didn't you tell me that before?"

The acknowledgment sandwich is the best way to help mold him into your perfect man—especially when it comes to smaller issues.

For example, you wanted him to hold the car door open for you. A great way to handle this would be to lead with appreciation: "I really enjoyed the night with you. I loved that you take such good care of me. I feel really like a Queen in a Queendom with you. And what would make me even happier is if you held the car door open for me. That would make me feel really special and safe and like you are my King."

As we stated, the acknowledgment sandwich is generally best for little things. For deeper issues, the open dialogue technique described above is generally more effective.

Reward the behavior you want to see more of. So whenever he does something you like or admire and that you want him to do more of, make sure you give him appreciation. Say things like:

Thank you, I really appreciate it.
I had a great time.
You're so kind.
You're such a good decision-maker.
I love when you take the lead.
I love when you plan things out.
You chose a great restaurant.

These kinds of statements will make him feel like he can be your hero, win you and make you happy.

That acknowledgment is so powerful.

Digital Communication

When you're dating, avoid texting and online messaging as much as possible. When it comes to getting to know someone or discussing important relationship issues, online messaging really is the worst, and texting is just about as bad.

Talking on the phone is the runner-up, and having conversations in person is the best. Meeting in person or talking on the phone is especially critical with deeper, more important, or conflict-oriented discussions. Avoid having any deeper conversations over text or online.

One way that you can encourage this with a man is to not text long responses yourself and to make any texts that you have to send as short as possible. You may also tell him: "I'm not a big fan of texting or messaging online. I generally prefer talking on the phone or in person."

When texting and messaging online, it's so easy to have a miscommunication and for things to go south. Also, the more you text or converse with a man online, the less motivated he is to meet you in person or talk on the phone. So you want to use these digital forms of communication very minimally. He can use them to invite you out and for you to say yes, but as far as details go, it's best to talk in person or on the phone.

Your phone should basically be used only as an appointment-setting device.

Research has shown that the online dating pool is full of emotionally unavailable men because they cycle back into the pool regularly. They date for a couple of months, then go back in. So if you're in the habit of messaging with a man, you're actually attracting these kinds of men.

If you do have to communicate digitally, don't respond to any message that's just a few words, such as, "Hi." If you feel the need to respond, just do the same back. Don't give more until he gives more.

And also, shorter is sweeter—and sexier. You want to give him just a little appetizer of the real, in-person you—that's it. Two sentences, and no more. If you send him emails that read like novels, he'll need to scroll back to the top when he gets to the bottom because he'll have forgotten what you said initially.

Most men will understand and appreciate it when you tell them that you prefer talking over the phone and don't like online messaging and texting.

And a reminder: Don't initiate romance. Let him reach out to you first. Let him ask you out on a date first. Just reward him when he does initiate by giving him positive energy and a positive response if you want to say yes to his invitation. Let him take the lead so you can create a powerful masculine/feminine dynamic that will quickly build attraction between the two of you.

Homeplay: Practice Being Captivating

Polish your captivating techniques!

Start practicing what kinds of questions you'll ask. Listen more and let him do most of the talking. Ask fun questions rather than boring ones. Avoid texting and online communication. Communicate in person. Practice the acknowledgment sandwich and the open dialogue technique.

Remember, less is more. And learn to lead with appreciation. Oftentimes, women are a little too much on the masculine, which can be emasculating. Instead, they need to allow men to help them. So practice being receiving. You want him to feel like the provider and supporter.

Reward behaviors that you want to see more of. So, when he does good things, reward him with great appreciation—a compliment, kiss on the cheek, hug, or acknowledgment of some kind. If you want him to stop a certain behavior, simply ignore it.

If you practice becoming a captivating, Queenly communicator, you'll attract a man to you, magnetize him, and be in a happy relationship very soon!

Chapter 8: Owning Your Pleasure

In this chapter you'll learn why it's so important to step into your yumminess, your deliciousness, and the power that you derive from the most sexual, feminine, powerful polarity essence you can be in: your pleasure.

This power comes from owning your archetype of the Lover. You could also think of her as the Seductress, the Siren, or the Marilyn Monroe. The power of this archetype comes from acknowledging it inside you and causing a man to feel the polarity—the difference between his energy and yours—which is an undeniably attractive vibration. This is chemistry.

What Is Pleasure?

Pleasure is everything that makes you feel good. Just imagine eating a piece of chocolate. Notice how your body opens up, eagerly awaiting this flavorful and decadent piece of sweetness. You can't wait to devour it. As you eat it, you're overcome with pleasure.

Pleasure is being in the present and filling every space of the moment with this energy. It's also leaning in, expansion, and relaxation. It's so juicy and delicious because it floods your body with oxytocin and many other wonderful relaxation and feel-good hormones that help women have more effortless and peaceful experiences.

Why Is Pleasure Important?

When it comes to dating and romantic relationships, Brody always says that a woman is the most attractive when she's in pleasure because that's when there's the most polarity. And that, for men, is the biggest turn-on.

When you own that pleasure inside yourself, you send out an incredibly magnetic energy.

What energy are you sending out to the world and to men? Are you sending an energy of pleasure, love, appreciation, happiness, confidence, sexiness, and beauty? Or are you sending out sadness, loneliness, bitterness, anger, frustration, and defeat?

When you reconnect with your pleasure, you take control of the energy you send out to men and the world. Men will notice you in a room and see you as a woman they want to spend time with. Over time, they'll want to be with you for life and absorb some of that energy because it's different from the masculine energy they have inside themselves.

Men have a lot of energies similar to yours, but owning your pleasure is what taps you into your femininity—and that's what creates the polarity and magnetizes men to you.

Pleasure fills you up if you had a long day. When you're in your pleasure, you can give more pleasure to others and receive it as well.

It's important to be able to access your pleasure because it's the lifeline between you and your man. It's hard for a man to access his pleasure because he's just not wired that way. A man needs to plug into his woman's energy and recharge.

How to Release Your Pleasure

Try letting your Lover out and reconnecting with her by yourself first. Become comfortable with her so that you can learn to let her out when you're around men. Come to feel confident and secure with that chemistry and energy. Own it without shame, anxiety, or fear. When you fully express it with the right man, he'll also feel the energy from you and want to express it as well.

Again, own your pleasure and be completely present with it. The man will be mesmerized because he can't figure it out. He doesn't know what you're doing or what you're feeling. He just knows that you're connected to something and he wants some of it.

There are ways to tap into your pleasure while maintaining your boundaries. We're not suggesting that you go out and start stripping or having sex with every man you come across. It's important to set boundaries and direct that energy toward good men you're interested in while still giving out the general energy to the world that you're a sexual being.

First, remember that pleasure comes from the senses. It starts with simply stopping. How many times do you stop when you walk down the street to smell a flower or watch a butterfly circle your head? You don't want to immediately whisk it away and say, "I want to be back in certainty." No, just be with what is. Open your senses and tune them in to the world around you.

Next, graduate into getting massages. We want you to practice this. When you get a massage—whether from a professional or your partner—fully surrender to their hands. Let go of your mind. Just allow your body to take over, expand, open up, and become more receptive and available to the juiciness. (Notice that we love that word *juiciness*.) It could also be just having a warm soft blanket on top of you. These are just more non-sexual pleasure practices that teach you how to allow pleasure in through your senses.

Finally, it's time to move on to sexual pleasure practices, which are our favorites!

Magnetize Your Man

As something really fun, we challenge you to smile with your pussy. Yes, you read that right. *Pussy* is another name for that most sexual part of you—your sacral chakra—because it has so much power. You can't focus on down there and not smile, because it's all pleasure. It's our life force. It's where life comes from, where our creativity comes from, and the place from which you can manifest your man. It's really, really important.

So imagine there's a smiley face where your womb meets your sexual parts. You can turn that smiley face on and you can turn it off. As soon as you turn it on, your environment will notice and you won't have to do anything else. Men have a sixth sense. They'll think to themselves, *She's connected with something. I don't know what's going on, but I'm feeling excited, and she feels a little exciting to me.*

Antia would just turn it on for three or four minutes while walking down the street and then turn it off because she got immediate responses.

If you can't do that or if you're not as visual, then just put your energy down there. Feel the energy in your sexual area, near your vagina, your yoni, your womb, whatever name or label you want to attach to that most sacred, sexual part.

If this is a little too challenging for you, then start with just swinging your hips. Swing them in front of the mirror to practice. Push them out in front of you then pull them back, and just play. Go to all sides and notice what you're feeling. Feel the opening of your hips and tell yourself how amazing you are and what a catch you are.

Touch yourself on your arm and slowly run your fingers up to your shoulder. Say to yourself, *I'm sexy and I'm the prize!* Swing your hips as you dance to music. A good song is "You Can Leave Your Hat On" by Joe Cocker.

If you still don't feel quite comfortable enough, then start with something a little playful—maybe just suggestively taking your jacket off.

We also recommend taking a burlesque dance class. This is very, very sexy. If you don't know what it is, look it up on YouTube. It's highly seductive and trains you to be in your tension. Burlesque has no destination; it's all in the process.

Another really good class is pole dancing, although these lessons can be athletically more challenging.

More Pleasure Tips

There are countless ways to find your pleasure and wake up the Lover:

Envision the Lover in you: What would she say? How would she dance? How would she move? How would she breathe? (Of course, she would breathe deeply.)

Seduce yourself: Fill a beautiful bubble bath and put on the most sensual music. Fill it up and stretch yourself.

Stretch yourself in other ways: Go outside your comfort zone. Do something you haven't done before or be someone you haven't been before. Feel a different energy.

Being in pleasure is not just an item on your to-do list. It's a very slow energy. The slower you can go with it, the more you'll receive and the more you can benefit from it, enjoy it, and fill up your tank.

When you have the opportunity to enjoy being in your pleasure, make sounds like, "Mmm." Close your eyes and feel free to touch yourself. Breathe very sensually. Swing your hips and own the world with your sexuality, sensuality, and pleasure. Add a little pleasure to everything you do. Incorporate it in how you walk to work, how you complete a project, or how you write. Really get into your pleasure as you take your clothes off before you go into the bathtub.

You can get into the Lover archetype by expressing sounds or words such as *Oh, yeah* or whatever sounds or words help you get into your pleasure.

Even if you feel uncomfortable getting started, breathe into it. This is your breakthrough, your secret gift to yourself and the world. This is your well that you can always fill up from at any given moment.

We facilitate and encourage this practice with the women who attend our Magnetize Your Man Retreats and on Antia's VIP Days. So, if you really want to practice these things, we highly recommend attending one of our retreats.

You can always start small. Begin by getting in touch with your sensuality. Start with what we talked about in Chapter 5. Fall in love with and tune into your senses: touch, taste, smell, sound, and sight. Start to understand all of the pleasures that come with those senses.

What are the most beautiful things you can look at? Go out into nature. Observe everything.

What are the most beautiful, sensual, sexual things you can listen to? Listen to a sexy song or make sounds with your own body.

What are the most sensual, enjoyable, beautiful tastes? Try different chocolates or flavorful foods that you enjoy. Try things that are just a little naughty and get you into that sensual, seductive energy.

Don't forget about sensual textures, such as soft, silky clothes or bed sheets. Learn to appreciate the luxurious feeling of stepping into a hot bubble bath. Get a massage or just walk out in nature and enjoy the feeling of the breeze on your skin.

Feel pleasure in an assortment of ways that will help you open up and be more receptive.

Adding a Man to Your Pleasure

Men are looking for a woman who can be available to their gifts.

They want to please you, and they want to know that you're receptive and will enjoy it when they offer you their gifts. Whether it's a kiss, a long hug or, of course, sex, they want to know that they can please you. When you're touching, kissing, or just being with a man, let him know when he does something that pleases you. Let him know with your voice and your body. Relax into it. If he's giving you a neck massage, for instance, say, "Oh, that's amazing."

Remember, we talked about rewarding the behavior you want to see more of. So, appreciate him when he's doing things that give you pleasure and show him that you're receptive to them. Be receptive to the Lover inside you. Be open to receiving when someone wants to give to you.

A lot of women we work with were taught to be givers. They help everyone but themselves. They bend themselves into a pretzel helping their children, their partners, and other people.

Now is the time to learn how to receive.

Once you can receive fully, you'll attract a man who wants to give to you fully. You'll attract a man who wants to be your hero, your king, your protector, your lover, your partner, and your friend.

Sexual Pleasure

When you can learn these things, then you can start moving into the more sexual practices, whether it's just pleasing yourself, dancing in front of the mirror, or using devices or toys that give you pleasure. It could be a feather or a rose.

It doesn't necessarily have to be a toy from a sex store. But we invite you to go if you haven't yet. Just stop by and explore to see if there's anything that you might like.

Regardless of how you acquire it, you can start with something simple, like a feather. Just feel the slight touch and discover what feels good to you. Is it a slight touch? Or do you like a little bit more pressure? Just really get to know yourself better.

Now, advance into the next stage. When you're in a bad mood, add pleasure to it. When you feel ashamed, add pleasure to that. Let's say you don't feel good enough. You can say, "Oh, I don't feel good enough. Oh, that's such a turn on." This is called a pattern interrupt. Your brain can't comprehend how you can say something that would naturally put you into a disappointed, self-pitying, depressed state and still flood your body with pleasure.

Start to rewire your brain by telling yourself things like:

It's safe to be sexy.
It's okay to be sexual.
It's amazing to be sexual.
It's okay to receive.
It's okay to feel pleasure.
It's okay to have greatness in life.
How good can life get?
How good can I feel?
How good is possible?

These kinds of questions and affirmations can help you bypass old blocks, traumas, or limitations. And then, of course, you need to actually do it. As you feel the fear, shame, and uncertainty, just break through them and feel the pleasure of that. Allow yourself to trust, feel open, and receive.

If it gives you an edge, you can remind yourself that you're safe when you do these exercises. Say "I'm safe" while you're swinging your hips, taking your clothes off just for yourself, or doing a burlesque dance.

Orgasmic Magnetization

You can also use orgasmic magnetization to connect with your pleasure. When you have an orgasm, tell yourself powerful affirmations, like, "I'm sexy. I'm the queen. I'm powerful. I'm a goddess. Men love me. I love men. I'm a catch!"

Usually, the affirmations should be short and easy to remember because, when you're in the throes of orgasm, it's obviously harder to get long sentences out. This is another powerful way to tell your subconscious that pleasure and orgasms are okay. Link them to positive thoughts and own these positive new beliefs in a deep way to manifest your reality, manifest your man, and start aligning yourself with your pleasure.

Homeplay: Feel Good!

So guess what your homeplay for this chapter is? It's going to be a whole lot of pleasure!

We want you to take on at least three ideas, such as finding yourself a feather, signing up for a burlesque class, and slowing down and smelling the roses.

You should push yourself by smiling with your private parts while walking down the street or going to the grocery store. Take any of the tools mentioned in this chapter and implement them for the next week. Have fun with them. Find out for yourself what feels good, how long it feels good, and how long you can hold the tension.

Connect to your pleasure any time you feel angry, disappointed, or just plain negative. Then add pleasure.

Here's an example. Antia encountered a woman at a conference who told her she was borderline arrogant. Thankfully, Antia had all the tools she needed to handle this. So, what did she do?

She just danced and told herself, "I'm so arrogant. Oh, yeah, I'm so arrogant." And just like that, her resistance to being arrogant went away. Otherwise, she would have manifested arrogance even more by resisting it. It was just the most amazing experience.

So, listen, we're not telling you to do something we're not doing ourselves.

No matter what level you're at, turn on some sexy music and do a little striptease in front of the mirror this week. Feel the pleasure. Pretend you're a burlesque dancer, a stripper, or a seductress. Watch yourself in the mirror and see how comfortable you can get with it. See how much pleasure you can give yourself and how turned on you can get while watching yourself in the mirror. Move your hips, get into your pleasure, and feel your body.

Again, if you haven't practiced some of the Lover exercises, take a bubble bath with champagne and candles. Put on some music and feel the pleasure with all your senses. If you can, get a massage or have a spa day. Take a burlesque dance class. Any dance class at all is going to be helpful because it gets you into your body. (It's also a great way to meet men.)

Also, take a walk in nature. Try to do it once a day if you can, or at least once a week. Go out for an hour or so and feel connected to the primal essence of nature. Notice all the colors and sounds. Really feel and be present because it increases your receptivity.

Practice smiling with your pussy. And, of course, when you're playing with yourself or making love to yourself, practice feeling the pleasure there. Get into your sexuality and tell yourself it's safe to be sexy and that it's great and beautiful and safe to receive.

Also, when you're feeling that pleasure, imagine that you're sending it out to the world and to every man. When you're having an orgasm, say short, positive affirmations to yourself. Imagine that you're with your ideal man, that he's there with you. Maybe imagine that he's the one saying the words. Connect to the deeper pleasure within you that he craves.

We hope by now that you're very turned on by yourself, by life, and by love. Have a lot of fun and a lot of pleasure. Enjoy yourself. We can't wait to hear how this goes for you!

Chapter 9: Trust

Trust and presence are the attractor factors. In this chapter, we'll teach you how to use them and draw your man to you at an energetic level.

Trust Starts With Yourself

So many women come to us and say, "I struggle with trust issues." That's why we'd like to discuss trust. What is trust and how can you grow your trust and overcome your trust issues? And what the heck does that have to do with being in the present?

Well, actually, a whole lot. First off, trust is, in and of itself, that sense of certainty inside you that another person will be honest, faithful, and dependable for you. You can even trust the world or yourself.

When you have trust issues, you actually lack trust in yourself, so you really have to try to discover where your trust issues originate.

Trust comes when what you think, what you say, and what you do are in alignment. So gaining trust is about taking everything that's out of alignment and completing it. It's like claiming you didn't eat the chocolate when you actually did. The issue here is that even though the person you told that white lie to might not know that you were dishonest, it's enough that you know.

Why? Because the lie forces a tremendous withdrawal from your own trust bank account. However, every time you tell the truth, correct a situation, or complete a project, you're actually making a deposit into your trust bank account.

You really want to think about that. What is it costing you to lie, especially to yourself?

It's taking away power from you. It's going into major debt. This is what translates into trust issues.

So, how do you align what you think, what you say, and what you do?

You have to understand what it is that you promised yourself. Did you promise yourself that you would go to the gym this morning but then didn't? Did you promise yourself you would complete a project but then didn't? Did you promise yourself that you would smile at a guy this time but then didn't?

You see, those are the building blocks of trust issues. Make amends with yourself by saying:

What can I do moving forward?

I didn't go to the gym this morning, but what can I do instead?

I didn't smile at the guy. What can I do instead? How do I make up for that?

Because you can still save this. You can still rescue yourself, but it's really the integrity inside yourself that's key. You'll become determined and connected with yourself when you begin to understand the impact of lying to yourself.

In addition to paying attention to lying, you also need to be aware of promises that you make. Have you made promises such as, "I'll be there at 7:00," but you actually arrive at 7:10? Or, "I'll help you out with this," but you never do? Many successful women have their plate full of commitments and suffer from *overcommitting-itis*, which is a symptom of a lack of boundaries.

As a consequence, you let yourself down and don't keep your promises. You overcommit because you don't set boundaries. The systems start to work hand in hand because they're interrelated.

Trust is a reflection and can be experienced in different ways. You may trust yourself at work, but not in your romantic life. You may trust yourself in your social life, but not in your family life.

To get in alignment and resolve trust issues, start by listing all the ways that you lack integrity, lie to yourself, cheat on yourself, or are inconsistent with yourself or others.

Here's the catch: If a men flake on you, lie to you, or do things you don't like, first look inside yourself and ask with curiosity and compassion, *Where am I doing this to myself? Where am I flaking on myself or flaking on other people? Where am I lacking integrity or not keeping my own word to myself or others?*

These can be hard things to reflect on, but it's so valuable to see that sometimes the things you don't like in others are things you can see in yourself. And when you discover these things, you can work to heal them. You could also work with us. We can help you work on and heal yourself so you stop experiencing those same issues with men.

When Brody and Antia met in Hawaii, Antia would say to herself, "I'll just swing by Brody's around noon and seduce him into some early lunch. Who cares about structure?"

But Brody would say, "No, I work until 5:00," even though he owned a business and set his own schedule.

This was an example of Brody being trustworthy with himself. He was true to the work commitments he made to himself. And because he trusted himself, Antia trusted him.

It's important to realize that trust is so much more important than being liked. In those moments, Antia didn't like Brody and was actually really upset over his refusal to sneak off for lunch—and she didn't like not being in control. But she trusted him.

You have ownership over your trust. Only you have ownership over your own integrity. And a big way to lose trust in yourself is to outsource your authority.

This happens when you ask others for advice, such as, "What should I text this guy back?" or "What could I have done differently on this date?" What you'll hear depends on your friend's personal perspective, their own internal views on dating, and their past romantic relationships. They'll just project their own representations onto you. So, be careful with advice from your well-meaning girlfriends. (As a side note here, always get your advice only from people who have what you want!)

How to Learn to Trust Yourself

How can you reinstate your self-trust?

Sometimes it's something you need to communicate. This is so important because it could be that you're holding something back, such as from your parents or an ex. Think about what it does to you when you withhold communication out of fear of not being liked or fear of facing an emotion such as embarrassment or shame. Think about what you need to communicate to someone important.

Make note of any trait or behavior that you don't like that a man is doing. Write it down and tell yourself, *This is something I need to look at. This guy said this. This guy did that. He lied to me about his ex. He wasn't authentic. He was weird.* Go on an internal quest to find out why you attracted this type of behavior. What did you do to create this experience or response?

That's what it always boils down to. When going deeper, you may be wounded inside or lack trust in yourself. There may be a gap in integrity within yourself. You may not be fully aligning with your values. Once you heal the gap and are better aligned, you'll stop attracting those things from men or other people because you'll put off an energy that doesn't resonate with that behavior pattern.

The Role of Energy

Men can feel energy from you. You might be wondering, *How does it all work?* Well, you project an energy. Even when you just walk into a room, men sense what kind of woman you are. Are you a woman who's out of integrity or a woman who's in integrity?

You attract to you the kind of energy you give out. Once you put out a different energy, you'll attract a different type of guy. You'll attract a higher-quality man. You'll even attract men who change their destructive patterns with you because you're in alignment and they unconsciously want to match that.

They'll be in integrity with you because they sense a level of healing. They sense that you've done the subtle emotional work that most women fail to do.

When Antia started doing the work to heal herself, she stuck to her own word. So every time she promised herself she would do something, she would do it. She knew she had to because she wouldn't know who else to trust if she couldn't trust herself.

So she went to the swimming pool when she said she would (and she got very fit). She made different agreements with herself and met those objectives. Men started being much more honest with her because she was being honest with herself and she gave off an energy of honesty.

For example, one guy she was dating told her before they became intimate that he was still dating his ex-girlfriend.

This kind of thing will start happening to you over and over again. Men will feel certainty and a high regard for you. They'll understand that you carry yourself with a high level of self-respect and are the Queen. They'll want to match it because they'd feel uncomfortable, even tense, if they didn't honor it.

Live in the Present Reality

Another way to learn how to trust yourself is to live in the present.

The majority of our clients have an anxious attachment style. So they sometimes live in the future, in anticipation land. They project all of their future expectations onto the man they're dating while he's blissfully unaware of their attachments and fears.

When you look into the future, you're just projecting shadows on a wall. You're guessing. You know that it's not reality right now and isn't tangible. But it can make you desperate, attached, clingy, and needy. It can cause you to have judgment and shame toward yourself because you know, on some level, that it's not real.

For example, if you knew tomorrow was Christmas, would you be clingy and needy about it? Would you say, "I hope tomorrow's Christmas"? No. You would just know that tomorrow is Christmas and be calm about it.

You have to make a whole lot of assumptions in order to live in the future. You have to make up a whole lot of stories to fill in the blanks. And you know, on an unconscious level, that those assumptions and stories are just your imagination.

They're an interpretation of your worldview that you have at that given moment, and it has nothing to do with what's happening in reality.

For example, let's say that after a date you called your friend to say, "It was great. He flirted, he's very interested in me, and he's turned on." This may not be true at all. It's the story you tell yourself and others, but it may not be the facts. Maybe what happened was that you met for coffee, you talked, you went home, and that was it. You need to acknowledge the difference between the facts and the story.

The story is how your subconscious can seduce you into making reality juicier and more exciting that reality. So, bring yourself back to reality. What actually happened in real life?

Detach From the Outcome

We learned from Wayne Dyer about the principle of the process versus the outcome. When you go on a date, you're in a process. The outcome is what happens as a result of that process.

Singles can get stuck in their dating, and a lot of them focus so much on the outcome that they forget about the process.

Women we work with focus on:

I hope he likes me.
I hope he asks me out.
I hope I get a second date.
I hope he proposes.

They become attached to these hoped-for outcomes and the process almost becomes irrelevant. The problem is they're engaging in future projection.

As long as your attention is always focused on and attached to the future outcome, you're not being present and you're basically losing your presence. You're losing your ability to be effective in the moment, to be a great partner, to be the Queen, to be attractive, to be interesting, and to draw a man in. You lose all of those things because you've thrown the process out the window and are focused solely on the outcome.

The key is to reverse that. Take your attachment and your desire and put them into the process. Say to yourself, *I'm going to show up as the best version of myself as I can. I'm going to be the best Queen I can be. I'm going to be present and enjoy myself. I'm going to have fun and be social. I'm going to be authentic as well as vulnerable.*

Completely let go and toss the outcome out the window. Let the cards fall where they may.

So be present in the now, not in the tomorrow. Take up the space of this moment and fill up that space in the Universe because then you're in the moment. That's the only place you can be in. You can't be in the past. You can't be in the future. You can only be in the now.

When you do that, you'll start to notice things more, and these may be things that are important to pay attention to. Maybe there's a red flag with a man that you would have missed if you were busy imagining yourself walking down the aisle with him. But if you're in the moment when that red flag goes up, you notice it and take action. We women have an internal intuition and guidance system that picks up on critical signals. That system is activated when you're in the present, but it doesn't work as well when you're focused on the desired outcome.

Don't be hard on yourself. In the beginning, being in the present is like a muscle that you work out. In the beginning, your brain will want to go into the future because there are bridges in your brain built to do that. So it's is important to break down the bridges and create new neural pathways. It can take a good amount of practice and time. Be gentle and kind with yourself. It may be a good idea to set some reminders on your phone that pop up to say "Presence" or "Commit to the process but detach from the outcome."

Being present also means letting go of the past. Antia has done her Magnetize Your Man Heart-2-Heart calls with over 650 single, successful women all over the world through our website MagnetizeYourMan.com. Over and over again she has observed that, as soon as she asks a woman what she really wants, so many of them just go backward. They say things like, "I don't want this to end up like my last relationship."

So, just be aware that your brain has a tendency to recreate everything that happened in the past. You have to make an effort to create only from the here and now.

The Past Does Not Equal the Future!

Before Antia met Brody, she decided that she wanted to be only with a guy who was between thirty and thirty-six years old. She was twenty-nine at that time. Where did that decision come from?

It came from the past because she had only met immature young men. If she had projected that past onto her present, she would never have given Brody a shot because he was only twenty-five when they met. But because she was coming from the present, she was able to see that Brody was actually much more mature than any other guy she knew of at any age.

When you come from the past, your brain deletes, distorts, and generalizes reality based on your past-based beliefs. Had Antia come from the past, she would have ignored all the moments when Brody acted very mature, and she would have distorted all the moments when he didn't act so mature. She would have generalized and said, "See? All men his age act like that."

The past isn't the same as the future. Just because you attracted a certain type of guy in the past or had relationships that went bad, it doesn't mean that it's going to happen again.

So separate the past from the present. A lot of women are living their past. Everything that's happening to them right now they're seeing through a lens of, *This is the way things are. This is what I deserve. This is what I'm worthy of. This is all I can expect. There are no good men out there. All men are liars, all men are* [fill in the blank]. They expect these bad things, so they keep living in that story.

You can write a new story for yourself by being present now and separating yourself from the past. You can say to yourself, *No, that was the old me. That was the past. That's not who I'm becoming. That's not who I am now. Now I decide to attract something different. I'm becoming the Queen. I have Brody and Antia on my side. I'm creating a new life. I'm creating new possibilities and throwing away the old story.*

Forgive those from your past and let it go.

Here's something that's very helpful. Do a Ho'oponopono prayer, in which you close your eyes and say, "I forgive you. Please forgive me." Imagine there's an energetic tie between you and your past, then imagine a blade coming down and cutting the energy ties. Just let the past go. Be open to your higher self and be free. Be in the present, but also have a vision for what you want to create. This will help you separate from the old stories and the old beliefs of the past so you can create something new.

Why is presence such a major attractor factor? Because when you're present, a man can sense that you're fully in your element, and he trusts you because you trust yourself.

The only thing that you can be certain of is this moment. Everything else remains uncertain, even the past.

Homeplay: Learn to Trust Yourself

Explore where you've broken agreements with yourself. Clean up agreements you've made with yourself, clean up any lies that you've told yourself, any incompletions. Then complete, complete, complete.

Write a list. Get a piece of paper and write out all the times recently when you broke a promise to yourself, when you were out of integrity, and when you told even a small lie.

Focus especially on your dating and romantic life:

When were you late?

When did you not keep your word?

When did you lie about yourself, hiding something or telling something that wasn't necessarily true about your life?

Write it out so you can look at the list and make an effort to heal. You could write a list of some of the things you hate about the men you've dated or relationships you've been in. Once you've written out the lists, ask yourself:

When have I done the same things?

What do I have inside me that I need to heal to make sure I'm not doing these things now?

This is a very powerful exercise.

Again, when you're on a date, feel if your feet are on the ground. Do you feel your back leaning against the chair? Do you feel your butt in the seat? Really make sure you're in your body and fully present.

Use the affirmation "Commit to the process and detach from the outcome"—especially when you catch yourself getting into the future. Whatever the results might be, whatever the outcome might be, let go of it and just focus on the process, being the best you can.

Or use other affirmations that will help you to get to a place of presence, such as:

Just have fun.
Enjoy myself.
Enjoy the process.
Let it all go.
Be here now.

Use these affirmations or the awareness in your body to get back in the present and out of the future.

Do the Ho'oponopono exercise to help you forgive, let go, and move into a healthier future. If you want to look it up, go on YouTube and look for "seven-minute Ho'oponopono."

It might help to write a letter of forgiveness to the people you need to forgive so you can let go and get out of the past. Forgive yourself, especially, for things that you felt you didn't do right or that you blame yourself or feel guilty for. Forgive yourself so you can be here now and look toward creating a great future.

Go out in nature, walk around, and be with the trees for at least an hour if you can. Look at the animals and insects and notice how they're present. They're not thinking about the future or the past. They're just doing their thing now.

Meditation is, of course, the ultimate exercise to help you be more in the present. Sit quietly and focus on your breath. Let your thoughts go and just be present with the moment. Look on YouTube if you want some meditation examples. Meditation music help you be in a trusting, present state as well.

That's how simple it is. We promise you, if you master these two attractor factors, trust and presence, your life will dramatically change. It will help you achieve a harmonious and powerful personal dynamic in romantic relationships.

Go ahead and practice. You'll be surprised at how much more open and available you'll feel. Feel that deposit in your trust bank account and how it translates into increased self-confidence. You'll find yourself more trusting with men, and you'll attract men who are honest, authentic, and real.

Chapter 10: Setting Boundaries Without Guilt

In this chapter, you'll learn how to set boundaries without the bitter aftertaste of guilt.

Look, if you're freaking out right now, we get it. Setting boundaries and risking rocking the boat was a terrifying thought for Antia. She gave her power away for the longest time—accepting when men called her later than they said they would, driving across town to meet them in their neighborhood, not speaking up when something just didn't feel right. The outer pseudo peace was more important to her than her long-term inner peace. She lost all self-respect, self-trust, and dignity. It caused a major conflict inside her that was reflected in who she attracted.

Boundaries are important in relationships because for a man to really see you as his long-term partner, he must like you and respect you. In other words, you need to be the Queen.

That's the beauty and the power of setting boundaries.

Boundaries and Why They're Important

First of all, it's important to be in your own energy so you're always congruent and coming from a place of choice. If you're not in your power, you automatically live and date by default rather than by design. Things are out of your control.

Second, it's important that you have balance. Antia says this so many times to the amazing women in our Magnetize Your Man Programs: "If you would just receive for the rest of your life, you would be balanced."

But the truth is that you're mostly likely already too overstretched. You've already given too much power away. You're too agreeable and too accommodating. Boundaries will help you come back into full alignment. When you're aligned, you're magnetic and everything flows effortlessly.

Boundaries are like setting a semi-permeable membrane around yourself.

We like the analogy of a country. A country can't exist without things (people, goods, resources) coming in and going out. If a country is closed off completely and nothing can come in and nothing can go out, then the country will starve and go broke.

But it will also die if it's totally open because it will lose all its resources to other countries.

A country can survive only when it has the ability to allow in the people, goods, and resources that benefit it and keep out those that would do it harm..

So, a boundary allows you to choose when to be open and when to be closed. It allows you to say yes when that's good for you, and to say no when that's good for you.

Boundaries allow you to retain your self-respect and give you power.

Boundaries also help you trust yourself. Many women who come to us struggle with trust issues that come from failing to say now and set boundaries accordingly. Boundaries will help you align what you think, what you say, and what you do. When you set them, you'll be congruent every single time and learn to trust yourself. And because we live in a mirroring universe, when you trust yourself, you attract a trustworthy man into your life.

Setting Boundaries Is Not Selfish

Society has incorrect assumptions about boundaries, and it places unfair labels on women who set them. There are many reasons behind this problem.

For one thing, if you're dealing with an energetic parasite, or vampire, then it's in their interest that you not have any boundaries with them. And when you do, they typically, don't respond favorably because now they have to source themselves.

And they won't like that. They'll think, *Let me manipulate her till she's right back where I want her to be*. One way they pressure you into pulling down your boundaries is by labeling you as a bitch for setting them.

Most women don't want to be called a bitch because a bitch is thought of as selfish.

That's right, selfish. People who benefit from you not having boundaries will tell you, "You're so self-absorbed, you're so egocentric, you're so selfish" just because you have boundaries to protect yourself.

In this chapter, we tell you how to change that dynamic. And when you do, it will be a metamorphosis, like a caterpillar turning into a butterfly. You'll come to say, "Yes, I AM selfish," and you'll celebrate that because it's healthy to have boundaries.

Boundaries are all about respect. If you don't respect yourself, you can't have a man respect you, and you can't attract a man who respects you. So you have to first respect yourself by saying yes to yourself.

Setting boundaries isn't selfish. It's actually the most altruistic thing you can do to take care of yourself first. You become more empowered, happier, and more contained in your energy. And as a result, you can bring that to the world and help others in a more powerful and effective way.

If you have trouble setting boundaries, chances are that you're imbalanced. We illustrated that with the concept of the King/Queen Matrix in Chapter 2. On the left side, you have the archetype of the Doormat, while on the right side you have the archetype of the Bitch. Your goal is to land in the middle, which is the archetype of the Queen. If you tend to identify more with the Doormat, you get into balance by adding in some of that Bitch energy, or what you might feel is Bitch energy.

Think about it this way: The people who call you a bitch or selfish are usually the selfish ones because they need your attention and they're trying to manipulate you.

How do you break through this? The main component is understanding that, by setting boundaries, you're actually doing the other person a favor. When you enforce your boundaries with them, you put them in a position where they feel uncomfortable and have to resource themselves. They'll have to uncover resources and faculties inside themselves, discover capacities, mountains of knowledge, power, insights, and wisdom that they didn't even know that they had.

Isn't this great? It's the biggest gift you can give them. In the moment, they might not like you and their ego will protest. But over the long term, it will be good for them.

This has happened to Antia many times. In fact, she once received a message from a woman she had set very clear boundaries with. The woman thanked Antia because, in the long run she found it truthful and recognized it as the path back to her own power.

So, you model that power by saying, "You know what? For me, this is important. I like you so much that I want to create trust. I want to create authenticity and transparency between us so much that I'm willing to not be liked in the short term."

That is what it's really all about. Are you willing to not be liked in the short term? (By the way, it's just one part of you—

your inner girl—who gets scared at the thought of not being liked.)

By setting boundaries, you create trust with others. And when you create trust, nothing can break it. The next time you say yes to someone, they know that you really mean yes, and that's an honor.

How many times have you talked to a person whose mouth says yes but whose body language says no? When you ask if they really mean yes, they insist that they do. What happens is you subconsciously trust the person less.

The same thing happens the other way around. When someone is truthful—when their words and boundaries match—you come to trust them more.

There's a famous saying: "You cannot help people permanently by doing for them what they could and should do for themselves." This is so true. And it's because when you turn yourself into a pretzel and sacrifice yourself for someone else, you're actually depriving them of the gift of stepping into their own power and becoming the best version of themselves. You might call it tough love, but it's actually real love. You help them become more empowered as you continue to show them your love and your well-meaning intentions.

Antia has girlfriends whose parents never set boundaries with them, so they don't know how to structure themselves or set guidelines in their lives. Trust problems are very common among these girlfriends. People might not like it when boundaries are set, but those boundaries create structure and trust.

Shadows of Boundaries

Many women also have many shadows inside them regarding boundaries—shadows they need to embrace in order to become the Queen.

A big part of embracing those shadows is to ask yourself, *Why am I afraid to be a bitch?* Honestly, be a bitch. Own that you're a bitch because it's the law of oneness. You're everything. As the song "Bitch" by Meredith Brooks goes, "I'm a bitch, I'm a lover, I'm a child, I'm a mother …"

It's really about understanding that you're everything and you're nothing, because out of nothing, everything can be created.

Here's the thing: You're not who you perceive yourself to be. So you might perceive yourself as a bitch while nobody else would. (Except the ones who know how to push your buttons.)

We have single successful women come to us all the time concerned that they're too bitchy. In reality, thought, they're people-pleasing like it's going out of style.

Labels Are Used to Control You

Hear us loud and clear: Lots of name-calling and labeling, such as "bitch," "selfish," "arrogant," etc. is used to control you.

Yes, that's right. The people in your environment subconsciously know that it triggers you, which is exactly their goal.

When somebody calls Antia selfish or arrogant, she just owns that. She celebrates it and maybe even dances a little, saying, "I'm sexy, I'm selfish."

Selfish is the new sexy. Think about it. How can you reframe it? How can you have fun with it? If someone uses one of these labels to describe you, you can be proud of yourself. That's because you set the boundaries when something was uncomfortable for you. So congratulate yourself! You're creating a new reality, and that reality is called being liked and respected at the same time.

Again, this is not a free pass to be compassionless. But don't be afraid to speak your truth out of fear it could offend people. Just speak your truth and then own whatever label they stick on you.

Having a man respect you is everything. But what does respect look like for you? Look into that for yourself and ask yourself what it means to be respected. Then ask yourself, *How much do I yearn to be respected by a man and seen as the prize?*

And as much as you yearn for that, you probably want to respect yourself, be true to yourself, and take a stand for yourself even more.

You should strive to do so unapologetically because it's your divine birthright. Your higher self is most likely resonating with this message. You feel it in your body. So we invite you to practice setting boundaries and earning respect. And you do have to put it into practice. It's a nice little concept, but it's meaningless until you put it into action. There's a great book Brody read years ago called *The Prince* by Niccolo Machiavelli, a renaissance philosopher, who said that it's far better to be respected and even *feared* than to be liked. What he found by studying politicians and leaders in all areas is that being liked isn't in your control, but being RESPECTED is.

You Don't Need Everyone to Like You

Somebody may like you one day and then decide not to like you the next day on a whim. Maybe they don't like the way you dressed or they don't like something about your energy, or possibly they're jealous. No matter the cause, it's out of your control.

However, people can't help but respect you for your actions because respect is under your control. You control that respect by setting boundaries, being the Queen, and respecting yourself.

Even if they don't like you or want to respect you, they still have to respect you because you're being a respectable woman—you're demanding respect through your actions, by setting boundaries, and by being the Queen.

Again, the goal isn't to be a bitch, evil, or mean to people. Instead, it's to practice being the bitch and being stricter with your boundaries so that you can get into balance and become the Queen.

Because when you're in balance, you actually get both love and respect.

Also, one of Brody's favorite sayings about setting boundaries is, "No is a complete sentence." This means you can just say no and you don't have to justify it.

The word *no* is enough justification in itself:

No, I don't want to.
No thanks.
I don't feel like it.
I don't want to.

That's it. You don't have to say why you're saying no. Excuses and justifications aren't needed.

Every time you say *because* as a justification, it's usually to justify your emotions. It's all made up. You may have no idea why your system felt a *no*. There will be days when you have endless energy and can take all the calls and solve all the problems. There will be other days when you can't do those things and you don't know why.

Why would you make it up? Part of your subconscious knows that your reasons usually aren't even the truth. Making up excuses will just take away from your self-trust bank account and, ultimately, from your confidence bank account too. Not to mention, the other person will likely trust you less as well.

If you say no to your friend wanting to talk to you now or to a guy asking you out when you'd rather take a bath or read a book, that's actually being of the highest service. Why? Because when you're in equilibrium, you have infinite capacity. You can reach a million more people with your energy level than if you picked up the phone or went on that date and let it completely drain you.

You're Like a Bucket

A good metaphor to think about is a bucket with holes. There's water being poured in, but every time water goes in, the holes let it go right back out. Think of yourself as the bucket. You're giving all of your energy to your children, your friends, and the guys you're interested in. As a consequence that energy just pours out of you and you can never be full. But if your bucket were all the way full, you could then fill up cups of water that you could give to people.

Where are the holes in your energy bucket? Where are you draining out your energy unhealthily with men and other people in your life? Why are you draining the bucket and not filling it up so you're overflowing?

Fill yourself up with love, joy, and energy so that you can be a full container of life force again. Do this so that you can help others and be a full container to give to the world.

When you do this, you'll also stop attracting men who have holes in their buckets. Instead, you'll attract men who are whole and overflowing. Together, you can build a greater world and a greater life of abundance rather than codependency or stress. We call these "power couples." These are healthy INTERdependent relationships.

How to Set Boundaries

By now, you might be wondering, *Okay, you two, how do I actually do this? How do I set boundaries? I don't even know how to say no. I've never even said no before. Every time I try, it just goes sideways.*

You can set energetic boundaries with people. Imagine that you can zip yourself up, like in some sort of raincoat. Imagine you're zipped into it and you're sending energy out and not taking anything in. It's like a raincoat because people's negative energy and attempts to drain you roll off you like raindrops roll off a duck's back. They don't get into your system. You can always send light, love, compassion, or whatever you want to send the other person, but you maintain your energetic boundary.

When you know toxic energy is coming at you, imagine there's an energetic shield in front of you and around you, protecting you from that toxic energy. It's an invisible boundary.

People tend to feel that shield when you set that boundary.

Here are a couple of additional techniques that work really well because they balance both kindness and assertiveness. When you use these techniques, a person won't even know that you're saying no. They'll think, *Wait, did she just say no or did you she yes? I can't tell because I feel really honored and so connected to her.*

Just think about what kind of aftertaste, what kind of after-emotion, you will leave the person with.

The Compliment Sandwich

The basic idea of the compliment sandwich is that you acknowledge or compliment the other person for what you like, then you state what you want or would like to have done differently. Finally, you end with another compliment or acknowledgment.

Step 1: Acknowledge/Appreciate Them

Acknowledgment is important because it's rarely a joy to receive a no. Just think about it this way: How would you like to be treated? Would you love to have a little comfort with the no?

Acknowledgment is saying "I see you, I connect with you, I see your gifts, I see your intention."

So when a man does something you don't like or you need to set a boundary, you begin with acknowledgment, using the phrase "I really appreciate." You could say, "I really appreciate this amazing dinner you made me tonight," or "That was a great massage you gave me," or "You're such an amazing, attentive man to find your way to my home to pick me up and then wait ten minutes." Just find something that's authentic to you.

Step 2: Deliver Your No

The next step is to state your desire. The easiest way is to say it simply, such as, "But I'm really not ready to sleep with you tonight," or "But I do have to go home now," or "I don't appreciate how you spoke to me just now."

Step 3: Give More Acknowledgement/Appreciation

Lastly, end with another compliment or another acknowledgment, such as, "Again, I really appreciate ... " and end it with pleasantness. It's like when you give a pill to a dog. You put it in some juicy meat, give it to the dog, and it goes down just fine. That's what you want to do when you're setting boundaries. Make it as pleasant an experience as possible. It will reduce any guilt you may have and won't feel as bad for the other person.

Homeplay: Say No

Practice saying no to your friends, your family members, and men. Practice different ways to express what would make you happy, what would make things better, and what would best help you.

Also, write in your journal or think about what it means for you to be respected versus liked. Because when someone respects you, the liking comes they you can better trust you.

If you're not used to it, practice saying no in front of a mirror. Practice breathing into the discomfort that might come with it. Just let yourself be with that tension. Don't feel that you have to justify it or explain it because, again, no is a complete sentence. You don't have to add any more to it when you're setting a boundary.

You can even visualize yourself saying no and setting boundaries in situations that have happened in the past or that may come up in the future so it's easier for you to do it if it happens.

Say no and let it resound in the cells and organs of your body. You may start crying if you experienced some abuse in the past or some overstepping of boundaries. All of it could come up—times when you didn't or couldn't honor yourself in the moment. If this happens, just open up to it and allow it to move through you.

It's just like house cleaning. It's cleaning out all the debris that keeps you from experiencing a better life, having wonderful relationships, and living the kind of life that you want to have with your man.

You might get angry. If so, let the anger out and say, "No, no!" Practice this. Get really get angry and get that emotion out.

Think of yourself as a beautiful castle or mansion with strong doors that keep the bad energies out and open up for the good energies. Turn yourself into the respected prize that quality men want to pursue and fall in love with!

Chapter 11: Vulnerability Without Weakness

Vulnerability is one of the biggest secrets to allowing a man to feel like you can be the woman he can see himself spending the rest of his life with, taking care of, being connected to, falling in love with, and staying committed to.

Vulnerability brings a sense of the unknown. It can feel awkward, it can feel uncomfortable, and to be honest with you, it can feel a little bit like a free fall—like there's nothing to hold on to. You have nothing to compare the situation to.

This was certainly true when Antia met Brody. She couldn't compare Brody to anyone else. She'd never experienced that kind of emotion or relationship before and she just didn't know how to categorize it.

This is a perfect example of what vulnerability is. It's the space between the notes. It's the space between the breaths that you take. It can also be the space after you say something really meaningful and you just stay with the emotion without any justification or clarification or, even worse, an apology. Vulnerability is standing in your power and just owning it.

It's is being authentic and owning your true self, heart, and emotions. It's standing 100 percent congruent with your emotions and not making excuses for them, not feeling ashamed, and not feeling like there's something wrong with you. It's just saying, "Yes, this is me, these are my emotions. This is who I am."

Vulnerability Is Not Weakness

Vulnerability does not mean that you're being taken advantage of, manipulated, or controlled.

As a matter of fact, we'll show you how, when you're vulnerable, you have even more control, are even more in charge of your own life, and are even more likely to attract a man you can trust because you trust yourself.

Why else is vulnerability so important? It will give you more power in relationships because when you're being vulnerable, opening your heart, and allowing a man in, he can connect with you. Love can come in because he feels safe to be vulnerable with you as well. He'll be able to connect to your heart..

If you've been attracting emotionally unavailable men, it's because you're also being emotionally unavailable either with yourself or others. Open up to allow a man to see and feel your vulnerability. It will make him want to be your hero, protector, provider, lover, and best friend.

Antia experienced her own vulnerability when smiled at men while being completely unattached to whether they smiled back at her or not. She was just being in that space and expressing what was calling forth through her without knowing how a man would respond.

Are you curious about how you can embrace vulnerability without feeling like you're week or giving away your power? Would you like to know how you can feel stronger and more empowered when you're vulnerable?

How to Step Into Your Vulnerability

First of all, look at all the emotions that you cringe at—the ones that you would never allow yourself to feel because you have a certain story or judgment around them.

For instance, maybe one of your parents was angry and you swore you would never be that angry, you would never abuse that power. Or maybe you have a judgment around sadness that makes you think you have to always be there for everyone else and that being sad yourself could lead you to being taken advantage of.

Whatever it is for you, that's the emotion to embrace and really start to feel.

Connect to the emotion that's coming up for you so you can move it through you faster and more effectively.

Remember: The word *emotion* means *energy in motion*.

How can you increase your emotional range? Because you might have two or three emotions that you play out over and over again, day after day, but there are many other emotions that you're not tapping into.

When you're vulnerable, opening your heart, and showing who you really are—including your fears, anxieties, sadness, loneliness, and discomfort—it's like a magnet for men. Because a masculine man, a strong man, will sense that and want to become your hero, protector, and provider.

You'll awaken that feeling in him of being needed. He'll say to himself, *Here's something I can be a part of. She's open and receptive to me. I can provide some value in her life. I can help her to feel safe, secure, and cared for.* He'll want to step into that role because it's the law of the Universe.

Vulnerability is also one of the keys to femininity, the receptive energy that attracts the masculine man who wants to take care of you. When you're receptive and open, you're allowing a man to want to take the leadership role.

You need to trust your power because vulnerability is not just the emotions that could cause you to lose something. It's also what could cause you to abuse something. So, the other side of the pendulum is the perpetrator. When you trust yourself to have all of this power, you won't abuse it.

Here's an example: When Brody and Antia started dating, at one point Antia said to Brody, "A part of me really wants to manipulate you right now."

Brody's response was, "That's interesting. Tell me more about it. How does that part of you want to manipulate me?"

Antia opened up to him and said, "I want to guilt-trip you, to make you feel bad."

So you also have to see for yourself how much you're trusting yourself to stay honest and act with integrity. You don't want to abuse the heart of your amazing man and do whatever you want with it. That's a big piece of your subconscious and a part of you that you might not be aware of. It requires the deepest work around vulnerability possible.

Also, you empower the man by allowing him to be vulnerable. When Antia was vulnerable, she empowered Brody to be vulnerable, angry, and sad. We're not talking about getting into drama and stories. But we are talking about being authentic. There's no one who's never sad. Someone who says they're never sad might not feel safe or have learned early on that their expressions of emotion aren't welcome.

When you allow yourself to marinate in this, to really feel it, guess what happens?

You can create! You can launch like a rocket ship because you have all the momentum. You have so much power inside you because you're no longer resisting.

You have all the energy that has been set free inside you. You can now utilize and channel it into creative projects, visualizations, ideas, or exercises. Whatever it is for you, you can utilize that fuel, that momentum, to your benefit.

The Benefits of Vulnerability

If you're really in your vulnerability, no one can attack you. You're in total control of yourself. If you don't own your vulnerability, everybody else owns you because you'll do whatever it takes so that they don't find out that you're sad, have a selfish side, or can get angry.

Let's say someone told you, "You're such a bitch." If you own it, you can just say, "Yes, I am. Part of me is a bitch and thanks for noticing!" But if you don't own it, then the other person owns you because then you go into attack, defense, justification, and shame, and this depletes all your creative resources and faculties.

When you're owning your vulnerability, you're allowing the other person inside. For example, we did a shadow ceremony when we got married. That means we shared with each other our deepest fears, insecurities, and judgments going into the marriage. Brody was afraid of losing his freedom in the marriage. while Antia was afraid to not be good enough.

Because we shared very sensitive facts and fears with each other, we got a good sense of the whole marriage—not just the hearts and roses parts. Going into a wedding, most people just look at the magical fairy tale on the surface. They don't look at the dark aspects that every relationship has. They push that away. But, if you embrace the dark, then you've got the whole yin and yang. You see the whole picture. And that means you can build your relationship on a solid foundation.

We shared our shadow vows with everyone present at our wedding before we said our actual vows. As we shared, many of our guests wondered what was going on. But once they understood that we were sharing both the light and dark aspects of ourselves, they let out a sigh of relief and loved it. We created depth, understanding, and authenticity that build a solid and lasting relationship.

Shadow ceremonies are invaluable to the success of a marriage. Even in the early dating stage you can do something like it, but it's especially powerful before going into a wedding or exclusive relationship. If you don't attract the right kind of man to do it with you, then, you've got to do work on yourself first. That's because the men you attract are a reflection of who you are.

Additionally, the relationship is a reflection of the emotions inside you. So, do some house cleaning first and ask yourself where you're afraid. What are you judging? Where are you repressing your own emotions and not really feeling or expressing them fully?

It may be that you judge yourself for being selfish. Try saying, "I love myself being selfish. It's awesome and it helps me so much. I can be there for other people and I can be there for myself. I can get all my projects done and I can be there for my kids when I'm selfish because I fill up all my resources."

Sexual Vulnerability

Before Antia met Brody, she would get furious if someone made a sexual joke. She felt personally offended. Her girlfriends would have been easily able to see that that was her shadow. She had to learn to embrace that she was a sexual being. Under the anger, she yearned to be deeply sexually self-expressed.

Of course, now she totally loves sexual self-expression. We want you to fall in love with it as well, because sexual intimacy is obviously a big part of vulnerability. Sexual intimacy is a powerful path into more vulnerability for you because there's nothing more vulnerable, nothing more naked than being with another person in that way. This is especially true for women because they're most likely on the receiving end sexually. The man has the penetrating role, and that certainly takes energy.

But the most vulnerable, the most open role of receiving, is the feminine role.

It's just like giving birth to a child: It's a woman's ability to hold that space, that void, that vulnerability. But, it can be a very uncomfortable place. Vulnerability is inviting you to fall in love with tension.

How to Spot the Lack of Vulnerability

Here's a great practice for you: Intentionally create tension.

Express a desire that you may have not asked for in the past. Do it for yourself and feel the tension inside yourself.

We're often attached to who we think we are. We're attached to our identity and the labels we put on ourselves when, in reality, we're nothing like that. We can reinvent ourselves in any given moment, which is another level of vulnerability.

But how do you know when you're not being vulnerable? When she's coaching our amazing clients one on one, Antia will ask a question such as, "How does that make you feel?" or "What happened?" A woman will often say something very vulnerable like, "I was abused by my father," or "I'm feeling really sad right now," or "It's probably never going to happen." Then, usually she'll follow it with a laugh.

This is a good thing to recognize. If you catch yourself laughing when you say something uncomfortable, you're releasing tension and blowing it off. That's often a very good way to know where you're not practicing vulnerability.

Here's another clue: If a man says something vulnerable and you reply with something joking or sarcastic, you're protecting yourself from feeling vulnerable yourself. And that pushes men away.

One way to reverse that is to catch yourself wanting to joke or be sarcastic. Instead, feel the emotion and breathe into it.

Try smiling while you're feeling it, or just be present. Whether it's with a man on a date or on a phone call, just practice holding it and being in silence. We often see women avoiding vulnerability because they can't stand awkward or uncomfortable silence. They feel they have to talk and fill the space to try to keep things going.

The Importance of Silence

Silence is actually one of the gateways to feeling.

Being quiet allows you to get in touch with your emotions, both in a conversation or by yourself. If you're just quiet—not thinking, not talking, not doing—emotions will come up. So, being in a quiet space and not doing or saying something to cover it up is a very powerful practice.

Write this down: "Silence is the gateway to my emotions." This is meaningful because talk most often comes from your head. It comes from a place of defense, protection, anxiety, and fear. Spend more time with the silence.

Because Antia came from an anxious attachment style, she now meditates several times a day, usually an hour total in about two or three segments. It wasn't easy for her in the beginning, but it has allowed her much more capacity to hold that space for herself and others.

What Are You Resisting?

Try to uncover what emotions you're resisting in your dating and life in general.

Are you resisting sadness or anger? Fear or frustration? That's the foundational question. Also, when you chuckle, just really check in and ask yourself, *Why did I just laugh?* Become curious. Was it an authentic laugh or was it incongruent? Was there something else that wanted to manifest itself through you?

It's the same with anger. When you get angry, ask yourself, *Is there anything else that wants to come through me?*

Whatever it is, let the emotion move through you. Sometimes, when Antia attends events and something brings up a lot of emotions for her, she may take a break and go into the bathroom or her car. She allows herself to cry her eyes out, but only for a moment.

Practicing and training yourself to express your emotions is very important. You're training your muscle, you're training your brain, you're training your body to let go.

Let the emotions flow without suppressing them with a dam. Feel your emotions fully, whether it's screaming or crying into your pillow, or screaming or crying in your car or the bathroom. It might be throwing a temper tantrum or punching your fist against a pillow. It's a great exercise to release anger, fear, and sadness, so just do it. Let it flow rather than suppress it. You'll be healthier and happier when your emotions flow. As a consequence, men will also be more attracted to your energy.

But if you're holding emotions in, they'll boil up and fester. Men will feel that. You'll subconsciously push them away. They may think that the anger is directed toward them when it's not. So, get the emotions out of your system. It will bring the power back to you, and you'll be healthier and happier.

Be the Mystery

Another way to develop vulnerability is to retain a mystery about yourself.

Let's say you're at an event and you have an interesting experience. You may want to immediately tell someone, but don't. Just hold on to it for a while. Don't run to your friend or text someone or tell someone and share it right away. Keep it to yourself and experience how it feels. Allow your body to talk to you. Hold the tension, feel the emotions of it.

A Queen holds.

When you practice this and can do it regularly, you'll create a sense of allure around yourself that will make people wonder what secret you know. Because you literally do have a secret. Let the ideas and any other emotional or mental patterns that come up inside you percolate.

Homeplay: Practice Being Vulnerable

Practice vulnerability by sharing with someone a deep fear that you have.

You can start small by just writing it in your journal. Ask yourself how you're feeling. Write something that makes you feel a bit vulnerable and then maybe share it with a friend, a family member, or, if you can, a man you're interested in.

Share how you're feeling. You can do this on a first date as well. Start with something like, "I'm feeling pretty good right now," or "I got a little sad today when this happened," or "I was feeling a little afraid when this thing happened." You'll know that it's vulnerable because it will make you feel uncomfortable to share it, and that's great.

If at any time you have strong negative emotions come up, whether it's fear, anxiety, anger, or frustration, find yourself some private space and scream into a pillow, jump on the bed, punch your fists into a pillow or the bed, or kick your legs. If you have other roommates or people around you that may hear, you can do a silent scream or do it in the privacy of your car or out in nature. Scream and let those emotions out. Move your body, let the emotions flow. It's much healthier and more powerful than keeping them in.

Also, journal about what's behind the emotion. If you laugh or get angry, ask yourself what's going on inside to make you feel that way.

You'll become much clearer and more congruent, and you'll start to trust yourself even more. You'll become comfortable with your vulnerability when you start to create an internal map inside yourself.

Vulnerability without weakness means knowing you have power and owning it for yourself. It's one of the big secrets to attracting and magnetizing the man who will share your life with you.

Chapter 12: Courageous Confidence And Flow

Congratulations! You've made it to our final chapter.

We hope that you've done all the homeplays and applied the principles you've learned in each chapter. Now, let's talk about courageous confidence and flow, and knowing when to lean in, when to let go, when to take the risk, and when to surrender in your dating.

Courage

Confidence is about believing in yourself and building up your value. It's about knowing that you're the Queen, that you're the prize, and that you have lots of value to offer any man who's lucky enough to be with you. Let's talk about these concepts to put the nice bow on all the work you've been doing and everything you've learned on this journey so far.

Courage is about making decisions from your heart and not from your mind. It's also about intrinsic confidence and believing that you are the source.

You are where the authority lies. You create your own reality. You are responsible for your reality

That's where confidence really comes from. It's knowing that no matter what, you create everything around you—both good and bad. It's not always easy to swallow this pill, and you may be thinking, *I didn't create that jerk in that last relationship. That was him*, or *I didn't create my divorce and all the bad things that happened in my life.*

Sometimes you may also think, *I didn't create this amazing thing that is happening, I was just lucky.*

Well, no. Actually, you did create all of these experiences. You just did it subconsciously.

By you taking it on and saying, "Yes, I created that. I am responsible," you bring the power back to you. You're no longer a victim. You must take ownership knowing that you create your own reality. You have the power to create your future.

You have the ability to create good experiences rather than bad experiences by believing that you have the power, and then owning that power.

All the greatest religious and spiritual teachings tell us this: You create your reality. Your mind and your thoughts create your experience.

By starting to accept that you're the responsible party in your life, you'll have the power to create an amazing life. And that's where confidence starts. You're the controller of your destiny.

From Victim to Victor

Ownership creates confidence automatically. Why? Because when you own it, you can change it.

If somebody else has ownership over your life, behavior, responses, and reactions, then guess what? There's nothing you can do. It just leads to lower self-confidence, which eventually leads to a sense of helplessness and thoughts such as, *My life is at the mercy of* [fill in the blank].

That negative energy, depression, sadness, helplessness, and victim energy push men away. Additionally, you end up resenting men, the world, your past, and yourself. We know it's very easy to get caught up in blaming other people, past relationships, the information you've received, the government, your religion, and whatever you give your power away to.

There's an old saying: "Would you rather be right, or would you rather be happy?" Oftentimes, people get caught up with the need to be right. Or they have limiting beliefs, such as, *I can never do this because I have this disability or limitation.* There's also this popular saying: *There are no good men in my city.*

People cling to these beliefs and the need to be right when they should let them go. Then they make these beliefs their excuse when things go wrong.

The problem is, as long as you hold on to these beliefs, you can never have what you really want. As long as you're busy blaming forces outside your control, you can't reach for the amazing things in life that you truly desire.

There's an old saying: "You have to let go of the quart in order to grab the gallon." If you can't let go of the old, then you can't grab on to something new. If you're still holding on to the past, your resentments, and your excuses, you can never move forward. So notice for yourself when you're giving yourself reasons and making excuses. Really, where in your life is it more important for you to be right than to be happy?

Let go and be willing to be wrong. Be willing to say, "Okay, maybe I was wrong. Maybe that wasn't why I never had what I wanted. Or maybe that wasn't what's been holding me back."

Stop blaming others or even yourself and say, "I'm willing to be wrong. I'm willing to do something new. I'm willing to look for and become something different and have new answers so that I can be happy."

This is very powerful in a relationship as well. Once you're in a relationship with your man, the goal is to not blame him for things and be willing to let go of petty things that you used to get angry about and take offense at. Be willing to be happy and have a happy relationship instead. Have a happy life instead of needing to prove others wrong and needing to always be right.

Confidence

Part of courageous confidence and flow is knowing that you have the capacities and faculties inside yourself to deal with any challenging situation.

Know that you have all the resources and utilize your feminine archetypes. When you have that knowledge and deep conviction, your self-confidence goes through the roof. You take more action, you take more risks, and you're more courageous because you know, that, even if things don't work out or if they don't go the way you want them to go, you have the resources, tools, and strategies to turn things around.

Why are we even talking about confidence and why is it so important? Because confidence, universally, is sexy. It's an attractive energy and trait. The more you feel confident in yourself, the more you feel ownership of your life.

> You're not a victim, you're a hero.
> You're the SHEro of your life.
> You're the Queen of your life.
> You're in control.
> You're powerful, valuable, amazing, fantastic, lovable, worthy, and deserving.

All of this energy goes out into the Universe and people feel it, especially men, and they're going to be drawn to you like filings to a magnet.

What's the title of this book? *Magnetize Your Man*. The energy you put out draws men to you like a magnet.

Confidence, sexiness, and attractiveness are all within you. You create them and you're the source. You're the star to the planet, the rose to the bees, and the flame to the moth. Put this energy out when going to a social event or Meetup, to a dance or on a date, or even just to the grocery store. You'll attract positive energy and men to you. This is why having confidence is essential.

Believe in the Good in You

The other part of confidence is believing in yourself and learning to control your mind so that you have only positive thoughts about yourself.

Why? Because so many single women are their own worst enemies. They criticize themselves and beat themselves up worse than any enemy could do. They do the most damage to themselves.

Stop yourself when you begin to criticize yourself with thoughts like:

> I look fat today.
> I'm ugly.
> I don't deserve it.
> He's out of my league.

Catch yourself and reverse these thoughts. Tell yourself:

> No! I'm beautiful.
> I'm amazing.
> I love myself.
> I'm fantastic.
> I'm gorgeous.

If that's difficult, at least start small by saying to yourself, *I can be beautiful. I can be good. I can be gorgeous. I can be valuable.*

If you need to start small, then work up to feeling comfortable saying more positive affirmations, such as: "Any man would be lucky to be with me. I'm the prize. I'm worthy. I'm a Queen."

It can also help to write down all the things you love most about yourself. Compliment and acknowledge yourself for things you've accomplished in the past, all the reasons why you're awesome and a catch. Write down as many as you can think of, even small things. For instance, if you like your hair or you have pretty eyes, write those down! Place the list somewhere so you can see it and add to it. Review it consistently to remind yourself of these positive thoughts.

Another way is to write yourself a love letter as if you're dating yourself or falling in love with yourself as a romantic partner. Write all the reasons why you love yourself. Look into the mirror and read it to yourself, then kiss yourself in the mirror. Say, "I like you, I like you. I love you, I love you," until you feel the real sense of love that you deserve. This leads to confidence and feelings such as, *I'm worthy. I'm good enough. I deserve it. Any man would be lucky to be with me. I'm freaking awesome. I'm sexy. I'm a Queen.*

Men will pick up on it too.

Brody has taught Antia quite a bit about confidence and she loves this about him. Every night they share gratitudes. Brody will say how grateful he is for Antia but then, right away, he will say, "I'm also grateful for myself."

When Antia hears this, she often thinks, *Wow, I can learn so much from this man.* How many people, especially women, are saying, "I'm grateful for myself first and foremost?" Women are often thinking, *I'm grateful for this person, I'm grateful for this circumstance,* versus *I'm grateful for myself.*

Also ask yourself:

Who am I?

What are all the different aspects within me?

Which part of myself have I been showing most of today?

Start relating to yourself differently. Remember that who you perceive yourself to be is not who you actually are. You may want to write this down:

Who I perceive myself to be is not who I am.

When you shower yourself with self-gratitude, you're encouraging the positive and confident part of you—the part that you may not even know yet—to manifest more.

The Flow

The flow is one of Antia's favorite topics because she so often hears questions like these:

Should I email this guy or should I just let it go?

Should I just relax?

How do I know what to do?

It's all about the law of balance because magnetizing your man leads to everything coming full circle. You're the most magnetic when you're in balance. In nature, it's called homeostasis.
So it's always about returning to balance. What you want to ask is, "Should I lean in or should I let go?"

Well, consider what you did last time and what the results were. Try to determine what brings you back into balance. Have you been mostly pushing your body forward and leaning in? If so, it may be time to just lean back and allow whatever's behind you—your chair, your couch, whatever it is—to hold you up so you can take a break. Have you spent more time letting go? If so, it may be time to take action and be proactive. When things are hard or challenging, the goal is to figure out where you're out of sync and out of flow.

When things weren't working out for Antia, she tried not pushing for them anymore. It was very challenging in the beginning, but she stuck with it. Once, she went on a trip with a man, but the relationship didn't work out, so she immediately encouraged herself to let it go. She immediately said to herself, *This is not flowing.*

We would like you to journal about the flow. What does it feel like to be in the flow? When did you meet just the right people at the right time and everything just felt like it was magically flowing?

When Antia met Brody, they were thrown together over and over and over again and it was so in the flow that it was easy. There was no effort on Antia's part. They were carried toward each other, and neither one was really analyzing anything.

So the flow is really about returning to that place and remembering when and how to let go. This isn't supposed to be hard. People typically have a subconscious belief that things have to be hard. They think that when things are hard and stay hard, the struggle makes the end result worth it. It's an old concept of having to work hard—and it's not just in the career world. We also often translate this old idea into romantic relationships as well. But the truth is, no, it shouldn't be hard.

It should just flow. If it's not easy, let it go and stop pushing. Just let go of the outcome.

Detach From the Outcome

Write this down: "Commit to the process but detach from the outcome."

Put all of your energy and effort into following the process and letting go of caring about the results. Doing so will put you in a state of flow so you can actually be present. You can be flowing with the process and have it be organic with a man without overanalyzing, getting anxious, feeling insecure, and trying to plan everything out. If you're doing those things, it means you're in the future. You're attached to an outcome or you're trying to get an outcome. You might be trying to get him to ask you out, ask you to be his girlfriend, or commit to you. These are all outcomes that you become attached to. You can still work for these outcomes, but you want to let go of your attachment to them.

The Bhagavad Gita, a famous spiritual text, talks about being detached from the fruits of your labor, and being committed to selflessly working and doing things in the world for others. But, it also talks about letting go of the results, letting go of the outcome and, by doing so, allowing yourself to follow the path to enlightenment. This itself IS enlightenment. It's when you're able to work in the world, give to others, and be your best self, but at the same time let go of caring about the results.

Here's the paradox: The more you let go of caring about the outcome, the more likely you are to get the outcome. So when you notice that you're beginning to get attached to outcomes, remember to let it go. Results will actually manifest right in front of your eyes at lightning speed.

Being in the flow is also being in the feminine. Think about the mindset you'll have to embrace to allow the flow and feel safe. Don't overthink things. Don't worry about the flow feeling weird or unpredictable. The logical part of you that wants to keep you safe will protest and you may sabotage yourself.

You've learned everything, you've been doing your affirmations, you've done all the work. Now it comes into manifestation.

This is just Universal law: What you focus on expands.

Another powerful concept is the compound effect that explains how to gain even more momentum. That yes energy is very powerful, so make sure not to say yes when you feel a no.

Maybe your girlfriend shows up late to pick you up for a party and you're tired. Maybe you had a stressful day. Opt on the side of not going to the party at all. If you go when you're not completely into it, you're most likely setting yourself up for a bad experience.

We've heard from clients who went on a date after a bad day because they'd promised the man the date. The date was not great and going made them feel even worse. Why? Because they went on the date in the wrong mindset and with the wrong energy. All they really wanted and should have done was take a bath and just relax that night. They gave into their fear of missing out.

So first of all, really learn to let go of the fear of missing out. When Antia first started this practice, she thought there was something wrong with her if she didn't want to go out. She's normally a social butterfly, but there were times when she just wanted to relax and read. But there was nothing wrong with her! She was just letting go of the fear of missing out.

When you feel strongly about wanting or not wanting to do something, your body is helping you come into balance and to manifest things even faster.

Don't go to a bunch of parties despite being in the wrong mindset just because you think doing so will result in introductions. You could just go to one party in the right mindset, which could allow you to meet key people who could introduce you to other amazing people, places, and opportunities. It may never have happened if you weren't mentally present and were just pushing yourself.

You may think at times, *I have to go to this event. He could be here, he could be there.* Let us tell you, you can't miss your soul mate.

Do you ever wonder if you should go to a party or not? Do you worry that you may miss your chance to meet your ideal man?

Look, Antia met Brody at an event and then, literally a week later, she met him at another event. Then, another week later she met him at a housewarming party. Even to this day, they still run into each other at grocery stores, buying the same things. That's why you need to let go of the concern that you'll miss him. You can't miss him. It's just not possible because you and your soulmate are on the same frequency. You're like planets orbiting around each other.

Your only focus is to be in balance. Get yourself into balance and let go of that scarcity thinking.

Follow Your Bliss

That's another powerful principle that goes along with committing to the process and detaching from the outcome—what Joseph Campbell called *following your bliss.*

You can achieve it by listening to the flow of the Universe and paying attention to what feels right. Where is your intuition guiding you? What is your heart saying?

Follow your heart rather than your head. Your head will get caught in an almost inescapable cycle of overanalysis, fear, and insecurity. Your head is already planning for the future and embracing scarcity mentality, but your heart always comes from a place of love and belongs to your higher self. Also, the

Universe starts to guide you when you're very clear about what you want.

Follow your bliss, follow your heart, listen to that voice inside, and enjoy the process. Joseph Campbell says when we follow our bliss, doors open where previously there were walls. It doesn't have to make any logical sense, but follow your intuitive nudge when you think things like, *I need to go to this. I don't know why, but I just feel like I need to go to this event*, or *I need to not go to this event. I don't know why, but it just doesn't feel right. I feel like, actually, I should go to this other thing.* Follow those intuitive hunches and start to enjoy the process. When you're there, you can just start to have fun and enjoy the process. It'll be easier to let go of the outcome as well. Start to bring that pleasure into the process.

What if dating, relationships, and even marriage could be simple, fun, and easy? What if all these things could be simple, fun, and easy for you?

Well, they can! So embrace it. Tell yourself, *This can be fun. This can be simple. This can be easy if I just choose to let it be.*

Homeplay: Confidence and Flow

Here are some homeplays for confidence and flow. And remember, it's about the balance.

Practice following your inner guidance. Do what you want if it makes sense and feels right. Go out, have fun, do things, and meet people. But if just doesn't feel right, stay home and enjoy yourself.

I know some introverts out there who are reading this right now and are celebrating. They're saying, "Oh, that's great. Now I'm allowed to take more baths!"

No. For you, it's the opposite. Get yourself out. Get yourselves outside your comfort zone because that's where you'll find your balance. Practice doing what your inner guidance tells you and keep in balance. Stay home if you want to stay home or go out if it feels right. If you always stay home, push yourself to go out. If you're constantly going out, switch it up, stay home, and relax.

Write that love letter to yourself! Write down and acknowledge all the things that you most love about yourself. Acknowledge yourself for things that you've accomplished. Repeat them to yourself while looking in the mirror. Also repeat, "I like you" or "I love you" until you really feel it. Then kiss yourself in the mirror while feeling love for yourself.

Remember, if you want a man to like you, you have to like yourself first. If you want a man to love you, you first have to love yourself just as much. If you want a man to respect you, you have to respect yourself. It all starts with you.

Also, pay attention to your thoughts throughout the day. Are you going to negative town or are you going to a positive park? Make sure that you're not going into that dark place and beating yourself up. Instead, treat yourself like your best friend, your romantic partner, and the lover that you never had or always wanted. Treat yourself well first, and that's how a man's going to want to treat you.

This will also help you with your self-confidence. Remember, it all starts with you and the way you feel about yourself. Opportunities are awaiting you!

Putting to Work What You've Learned

As we come to the end of this book, we'd like to emphasize how important it is that you implement and practice what you've learned.

Dating and romance are a never-ending journey. It's a master's journey. There are always more things to learn and more refinements you can make. Studies show that if you're not as happy as you could be in your romantic life, it's very hard to be happy in general. Conversely, if your romantic life is fulfilling and happy, it's very hard for that not to translate into your overall happiness as well. Even if other things in your life aren't working, if your romantic relationship is tight and amazing, that makes everything better.

Keep on track with all you've learned and strive for the best. Inspire yourself. Be an inspiration to others in your life and to your children if you have them. Continue to use this book as a resource and review it often. Take any of the chapters that may be a bit more challenging for you and concentrate more on those areas that you need to work on.

Also, truly make an effort to practice the homeplays. All of the information in this book is designed to help you recognize the blind spots where you delete, distort, and generalize your reality. If you don't correct these blind spots, you'll stay exactly where you are and won't magnetize your perfect man.

You need to break through your resistance and open yourself up to a happier, more fulfilling life. Reviewing and implementing what you've learned and practicing the homeplays is absolutely essential. If nothing changes, nothing changes. And without new action, you won't get new results.

Stay committed to your vision and the goals that keep you taking steps toward your new, happier, more fulfilling life no matter what. Avoid that old scarcity mentality and concentrate on keeping an abundance mentality. Know that there are more than enough good men to go around, and one of them will be the one that you magnetize!

Your Next Steps

If you've loved and gotten a lot out of this book, feel free to share it with other women who could also benefit from this knowledge. It may even be helpful to you to have an "accountability sister," someone who takes the journey with you.

There's always another level to achieve and another journey to take. Your next step may be to reach out for additional, customized support, encouragement, and tools so you can continue to build your confidence and ensure success.

Antia has helped thousands of successful, single women all over the world find their best, most confident selves and learn and hone skills that ensure romantic success. Her clients have gotten married and are living happily ever after. A complimentary Magnetize Your Man Heart-2-Heart call with Antia can also help get you on the right track to having the life you've always dreamed of. She can guide you in the right direction, set up further positive steps to take, and direct you to new opportunities.

To claim yours for <u>FREE</u> as a special bonus that comes with this book, simply go to **MagnetizeYourMan.com** and enter your name and email, then select the best time for you, as spots are still available!

We're so grateful to have had the opportunity to help so many women achieve the happiness they desire and deserve. We've been invited to many weddings, and are always excited when clients send us photos of their babies or their new engagement rings.

We're looking forward to supporting you on your journey and are hoping to share the excitement of your wedding or any other event that may take place as you move forward. Please keep us updated on your progress and feel free to send us your story and let us know how you met your man!

You can contact us any time by emailing us at Support@MagnetizeYourMan.com.

We're so grateful that you've been a part of this journey and that you've taken your first step toward your happy romantic future by reading this book and implementing what you've learned.

You can do this. We're here for you and we look forward to talking to you more soon!

With much love and to your commitment to having lasting love in your life quickly and without fear,

Antia & Brody Boyd

~Dreams Can Come True~

Made in the USA
Las Vegas, NV
26 November 2023